COLLINS
HOME GUIDE

DECORATING
IDEAS

JANE CHURCHILL
AND
ANNIE CHARLTON

HarperCollins*Publishers*

This edition published 1997 by
HarperCollins*Publishers*

Created exclusively for HarperCollins by Amazon Publishing Ltd
Designer: Jerry Goldie
Editor: Susie Bihar
Photography: John Freeman
Text and illustrations © HarperCollins 1993

The text and illustrations in this book were previously
published in *Decorating Ideas* by Jane Churchill and Annie Charlton

A catalogue for this book is available from the British Library

All photographs by John Freeman

ISBN 0 00 414 004 4

Colour reproduction in Singapore, by Colourscan
Printed and bound in Hong Kong

Jane Churchill

Jane Churchill is one of Britain's leading interior designers. She started her own business
at the age of 21 when she opened a gift shop called Treasure Island in London's
Pimlico Road, having previously worked for Colefax & Fowler. She began taking on
decorating commissions, and in 1982 re-opened as Jane Churchill Design, offering
her own range of fabrics and wallpapers. In 1989 she sold her business to Colefax & Fowler,
and has since built up her own independent decorating business.

Annie Charlton

With over 25 years of experience and knowledge, Annie Charlton is one of the
UK's leading interior designers. Her professional careeer began in 1968 at Charles Howard,
Interior Designers and by 1986 she had become sole proprietor of
Sloane Decorators in Pimlico.

The publishers would like to thank Jennifer Jones and Helen Dickenson
who wrote the introductions to the projects.

Jennifer Jones

Jennifer Jones is a freelance editor and writer, specializing in the areas of
interior design, crafts, gardening and cookery. Over the years she has worked
with a wide range of authors, including Rosie Fisher on *Decorating Children's Rooms*,
Patricia Seligman on *Painting Murals*, and Jane Churchill on the *Collins
Complete Book of Soft Furnishings*.

Helen Dickenson

Helen Dickenson is a producer and director for Pineapple Productions.
She makes feature programmes for television, specializing in programmes
about interior design and decoration. She is the author of a number of
very successful information fact sheets.

Contents

Print Rooms

The print room was a form of interior decoration that was briefly popular in Europe in the late eighteenth century. Usually, the prints were pasted directly onto the wall and were grouped together in symmetrical arrangements. Religious subjects, pastoral scenes, contemporary portraits and classical figures were all displayed together. Each print was framed with a paper border and decorative elements, such as *trompe-l'oeil* swags, ropes, chains and corner-pieces, were added.

Reproductions of eighteenth-century prints and print-room decorations are now available from specialist outlets, bringing it within reach of the enthusiastic amateur. But if you do not want to buy a specialist kit, you can always photocopy prints from magazines and catalogues.

Before you start work, make sure the surface is matt, or the prints will not stick. A background in earthy colours such as terracotta or yellow ochre looks most attractive with antique prints. If you would like your black-and-white prints to look old,

soak them briefly in a bath of cold tea (experiment first with a corner of a border for soaking time and depth of colour).

Displaying prints

When it comes to arranging the prints, always start at the centre of the area you are decorating and work your way out. In the eighteenth century, size was more important than subject matter, and the largest print was usually placed in the centre of any grouping. You will need a plumb-line and spirit level in order to establish the true centre: carefully mark the central print, then start pasting down. If you like, before you stick the prints down permanently, use re-usable adhesive to position them correctly. As you work outwards, it is essential to keep checking that everything is aligned.

Successfully creating an entire print room requires a good eye and a great deal of patience. For your first project, it is a good idea to limit yourself to a small area such as a bathroom or cloakroom.

You will need:

➢ Plain, painted wall

➢ Print-room kit or photocopied prints from magazines and books, and ornamental paper cut-outs and borders available from art and craft shops

➢ Tape measure

➢ Spirit level (optional)

➢ Small pair of scissors

➢ Re-usable adhesive

➢ Pencil

➢ Wallpaper paste

➢ Paintbrush (to apply paste)

Method

1 If you are not using a print-room kit, choose your prints from magazines, catalogues or books. When photocopying them, make sure you use a high-quality paper. Usual photocopying paper may bubble when the wallpaper paste is applied.

2 Cut out your print borders and any ornamental bits and pieces you want to use. You will need a small pair of scissors, such as nail scissors, to cut out the intricate ornamental pieces (fig A).

3 Mark with a pencil where you want to stick the prints on the wall. To ensure you align the prints correctly, measure the size of each print and then measure in from the corners of the wall. Check with a spirit level, too.

A

B

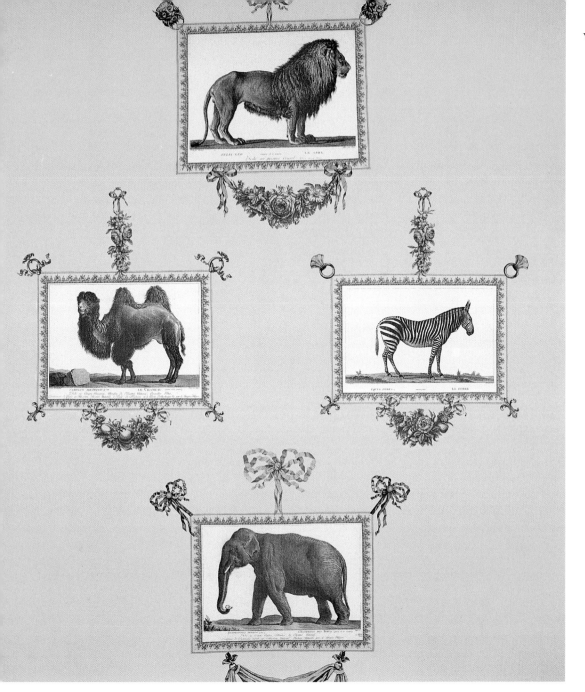

MORE
IDEAS

*Use prints and print-
room embellishments
to decorate other
items, such as
cabinets, trunks, boxes
and screens.*

4 Attach the prints with re-usable adhesive. Check they are
aligned properly. Once you are happy with the arrangement,
glue them on with wallpaper paste.

5 Stick the cut-out borders over the prints. If you are not using
a kit, you will have to cut the borders into four pieces and
mitre the joints. (A mitred joint is a right-angled corner formed
by two strips of material joined together, each having an edge cut
at a 45° angle.) To mitre the print borders, fold over the top and
bottom of each side border at a 45° angle, then cut off the end
(**fig B**).

6 Place the ornamental bits and pieces around the frame.
When you are happy with the effect, paste them on (**fig C**).

C

Pleated Fabric Wallhanging

As far back as the Ancient Greeks, and until the introduction of mass-produced wallpapers in the nineteenth century, hanging fabric on walls provided not only decoration but also a measure of insulation and sound-proofing. As fabric coverings also disguise poor wall surfaces, they were invaluable before the days of the plastered wall. The method favoured by the Greeks and Romans was to fix fabric to the top of the wall and then let it hang down loosely. Their brightly woven or embroidered pieces were supple enough to be gathered and draped around the room and over doorways. In contrast, in the Middle Ages, substantial tapestries were fashionable and these were hung from rings on a rod or from wooden pegs.

Fixing fabric directly to walls first became fashionable during the seventeenth century and by the eighteenth century it was the most common method used for covering walls. These days, some fabrics come with a paper backing so that they can be stuck directly to a surface. They include wools, cottons, felts, silks and moirés, and suedes. Wools and silks also come in textured forms; coarser textured wall coverings include hessians, jutes and linens. If you use ordinary, unpapered fabric, you will need to screw wooden battens to the wall first to which the fabric can then be secured with nails or staples.

If you intend to gather or pleat the fabric, each join can be neatly hidden behind the previous pleat. Or you can make a neat box-pleat as shown in the project. If you are working with a patterned fabric, make sure you match up the pattern. Always finish with a trimming of braid to hide the nails or staples.

You will need:

- A piece of fabric the length, and twice the width, of the wall you wish to cover
- Tape measure
- Enough braid to frame the wall area
- Staple gun
- Sewing machine
- Fabric glue

Method

1 Measure the length and width of the wall area you intend to cover.

2 Cut a piece of fabric to the appropriate size (this should be about half of the fabric you have bought). If you have a dado rail, it is better to cover just the area of wall above it. Unless you are confident of your ability, do not choose a patterned fabric such as a check – matching up the squares may cause you problems later on.

3 Staple the fabric you have cut out to the wall at the top and bottom **(fig A)**. You will probably need someone to hold the other end of the fabric as you staple.

4 You need to make 10 cm (4 in) strips to cover the wall, leaving a 10 cm (4 in) gap between each strip. Once you have measured the width of the wall, calculate how many strips you require. To make the strips, cut out double the width of the finished strip. With each strip fold the ends over to make a hem

A

B

C

and machine. Then fold the strip in half, with the wrong side showing. Machine down the edge and then turn the good side out. Once you have made the strip, press the seam so that it lies down the centre back.

5 Leaving 10 cm (4 in) between them, staple on the strips at the top and bottom of the wall (fig B). In addition to stapling the strips at the top and bottom, you may need to glue them in the centre to stop them sagging.

6 Measure and cut lengths of braid to run across the top and bottom of the wall area, and two for the sides. Glue the braid over the top, bottom, and side edges of the wall area to cover the staples (fig C). Mitre the corners (see page 5).

MORE IDEAS

Calico is a very inexpensive fabric for covering walls. The traditional colour is cream, but some outlets stock calico in a range of colours.

If you have a limited budget, introduce a dado rail (see pages 12–13). Cover the area above the rail with fabric and use paint on the wall below.

Painted Tiles

Decorative wall tiles date back to hundreds of years B.C., when they were first used by the Egyptians to adorn their temples and tombs. Over the centuries, different countries developed their own particular designs, shapes and uses for tiles. In Holland, blue-and-white Delftware tiles were put behind beds, on staircases and around window frames, while in America, large tiles were used in the hallways of grand buildings. Italian craftsmen produced a very different effect by covering their tiles in wonderful transparent glazes. In Victorian Britain, it was fashionable to have individual family portraits painted onto tiles, while in France, seascapes, often in painted in yellow with a blue background, were preferred. As well as being highly decorative, tiles are, of course, eminently practical. As they are adaptable, cool and easy to clean, they are particularly popular in hot countries, especially Spain and Portugal.

For practical purposes, tiles are often used as wall coverings between units in kitchens and bathrooms. An attractive idea for a kitchen wall is to dot single decorated or picture tiles at random among plain ones or to arrange a group of tiles to form a mural.

You can easily paint plain white tiles yourself, either singly or in a group to form a mural. However, it is important to remember that because they haven't been fired in a kiln, your own painted tiles will not stand up to being scrubbed. Before you begin, clean them using a damp cloth. If you are not particularly confident about painting, use a stencil or create a simple pattern in spots or stripes, which can then be used as a border. If you intend to paint free-hand, draw the design in pencil before you apply the paint – the pencil markings can be rubbed out when you have finished. A clever idea for a kitchen is to paint individual tiles with objects that you or your family particularly like. This could be anything from a jar of jam to a ladybird. One of the most popular designs for painted tiles is the Delft look, which originated in Holland. In the following project four plain white tiles are painted to form a mural of a blue-and-white jug.

You will need:

- Four plain white wall tiles
- Pretty blue-and-white jug or other piece of china to copy (or a photograph of one)
- 0.5 lt (1 pt) of warm water
- Two teaspoons of vinegar
- Piece of paper as large as the four tiles, divided by pencil lines into four quarters and then into a grid of 2.5 cm (1 in) squares
- Chinagraph or soft pencil
- Small jar of dark blue ceramic paint
- Artist's brush, no 5
- White spirit to thin the paint
- Saucer for mixing paint with white spirit

Method

1 On the grid paper, draw the outline of the jug and draw the designs inside the outline. These can be as simple or intricate as you like (fig A).

2 Mix the vinegar and water and use to wash the tiles. Dry the tiles thoroughly.

3 Arrange the tiles in a square on a flat surface. You may need to use double-sided sticky tape underneath to keep them in place while you work on them.

4 With a soft pencil or chinagraph draw the grid and the outline of the jug onto the tiles (fig B).

5 Using the blue ceramic paint and the artist's brush, paint the outline of the jug over the pencil line.

6 Again, using the artist's brush, with the grid drawing as a guide, paint the decoration inside the outline. It is a good idea to paint some of the decoration in a paler blue, which you can achieve by mixing some of the paint with a little white spirit in a saucer (fig C).

7 Leave the tiles to dry for at least a week. Once they are dry, gently rub out any pencil or chinagraph marks that are showing. When attaching these tiles to a wall, it is better to use a tile-fixing adhesive rather than grouting, so that the tiles can be pushed together and the design is kept intact.

A

MORE IDEAS

❖

Alphabet tiles are a great idea for your child's room or a bathroom. They are just as educational as blocks, and will not end up littering the floor.

❖

If you are hand-painting plain tiles to use as a border, remember to buy tiles with rounded edges.

Lemon Tree Mural

Creating a mural is enormous fun and a great way to allow your artistic side full rein. This does not mean you need the technical and artistic virtuosity of a Michelangelo – a mural can be as simple as painting a colourful rainbow to frame the door of a child's bedroom, or as small in scale as a trellis covered in climbing plants in an alcove area. Murals do not have to be confined to wall surfaces either. Doors and cupboard doors are perfect for this treatment and provide a useful framework within which to work.

The secret to a successful mural is to keep everything simple. Some of the most beautiful and striking examples of murals are the wall-paintings that adorn the tombs of the Ancient Egyptians and Etruscans, the palaces of Crete and Roman villas. These murals show stylized images of both plants and animals on plain or abstract backgrounds, often with patterned borders. There is always a stunning use of colour.

Whilst these ancient murals provide inspiration, when attempting your first mural you may like to choose a more modern theme. In a child's room, you could paint a blustery sky with clouds and brilliant patches of blue along one or more walls. The sky can then be filled with anything from colourful balloons and kites to your child's favourite fairy-tale or cartoon characters. It is a good idea to paint these separately onto paper or card and stick them onto the wall – this makes them easy to replace as your child's tastes change. In a small dining room or in a corridor, a series of stylized lemon trees in pots, as shown in the following project, perhaps alternating with orange trees, is very attractive. A decorative border above and below the trees will clearly define the space. You can either stencil on your border or you can stick down one of the many excellent ready-made border papers that are available.

A completely different use of mural work is *trompe-l'oeil*, the art of tricking the eye. The idea is to create a three-dimensional effect on a flat surface. To be truly effective, however, this work is probably best left to the professional.

In the following project, you are shown how to paint a stylized lemon tree. This can either stand alone or be part of a frieze.

You will need:

Plain painted wall or a wall hung with lining paper

Pencil

Stiff paper or cardboard for stencils

Scissors

Masking tape

Stencil brush

Ruler

Medium-sized tube of yellow acrylic paint

Medium-sized tube of brown acrylic paint

Medium-sized tube of green acrylic paint

Method

1 Prepare the wall area. If you are going to paint the mural directly onto the wall, you will need to clean the wall surface first. Or, if you like, you can cover your wall in lining paper, and paint the mural onto this. Obviously the size of the mural depends on the size of the wall. However, you should follow these dimensions: the pot should be smaller than the tree top; the stem should be about three times the height of the tree top. The width of the stem should be about 5–7.5 cm (2–3 in) depending on the size of your tree. Altogether, your mural should be two thirds the height of the wall.

2 Next make the stencils. You will need to make stencils for the lemons, the pot and the leaves. To make your lemon stencils, draw on paper three different sizes of lemons. Then cut out the shapes. If you like, you can copy real lemons. Make the leaf stencils in the same way. An excellent way of drawing the pot outline is to take a sheet of paper and fold it in half. Draw the shape of half a terracotta pot. Cut out the pot shape and open out the paper.

3 Attach your pot stencil to the wall with masking tape. Paint inside the stencil with the yellow acrylic paint. Leave it to dry. Then, with the stencil brush, stipple over the yellow in brown acrylic paint, allowing the yellow to show through **(fig A)**. To stipple, dip the brush lightly in the paint, hold the brush at right angles to the wall and dab the paint on. Do not press too hard.

4 Measure your stem length and width with a ruler and mark it in with pencil.

5 Now, start on the lemon stencils. Hold a stencil against the wall and stipple with the stencil brush using the yellow acrylic paint. Do not put too much paint on the stencil brush as it may drip. If the stencils get a little soggy, let them dry out before you continue.

6 Stick masking tape down the stem outline and with the stencil brush paint with brown acryllic paint. When it is dry (it should only take a few minutes) peel off the masking tape and free-hand, with a small paintbrush, paint in the little stem shoots **(fig B)**.

7 Now turn your attention to the leaves. Using green acrylic paint, stencil them in the same way as the lemons **(fig C)**.

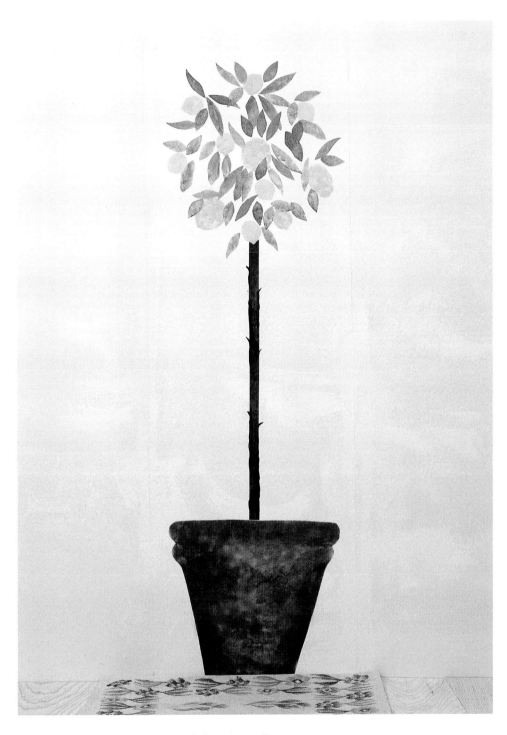

MORE IDEAS

*A mural can be created in a variety of mediums. Stencils,
rubber stamps or home-made vegetable prints
(see pages 26–27) are all suitable.*

❖

A plain door at the end of a long corridor is a perfect site for a mural.

Panelling Plain Doors

There is so much more you can do to give a stylish finish to walls than cover them with wallpaper or paint. By introducing mouldings to form dado rails and panelled areas, a wider range of decorative treatments becomes possible. But the application of mouldings does not stop there. They can also be used to transform plain doors, cupboard doors, shelving, mantelpieces and furniture.

In eighteenth-century Europe, delicate and elaborately carved mouldings were used to divide walls into a series of panelled areas, which were sometimes further divided by dado rails. Doors were also divided into panels, echoing the decoration of the walls. The walls were often painted in two or three tones of colour. In very grand rooms the mouldings were picked out in gold or in a lighter toning shade. A similarly elegant arrangement was favoured in the Neo-classical schemes introduced towards the end of the eighteenth century. All the architectural wall decorations – a cornice or stucco-work frieze at the top of the wall, panelling and dado rail – were generally left white against a plain-coloured background. This treatment works just as well in a modern room, particularly if it is rather box-like. By keeping the panels as upright rectangles, the eye is drawn upwards, giving an illusion of height.

Modern mouldings

Modern wooden mouldings can be found in most hardware stores. You may want to buy a plumb-line to help you get the lines absolutely straight. You will also need a mitring block for sawing corners. Paint the areas within the panels either a tone lighter or darker than the main wall colour, and the moulding in a complementary colour.

In the eighteenth century chairs were placed against the wall, so a rail at chair height protected expensive wall decorations from scrapes and bumps. Nowadays, the dado rail is useful along the length of a staircase, which often gets scuffed, with the wall above papered and the area below the rail painted off-white or to tone in with the wallpaper.

Absolutely plain doors are transformed when decorated with mouldings: use them to introduce panels, such as a pair of rectangular panels positioned above two smaller square or rectangular panels. Mouldings can also be used on plain cupboard doors to great effect.

You will need:

- Plumb-line or tape measure
- Pencil
- Wooden rope moulding
- Small mitring block
- Small handsaw
- Re-usable adhesive
- Wood glue
- Filler
- Scraper (to apply filler)
- 0.5 lt (1 pt) tin of eggshell paint

Method

1 In this project, we have made a rectangular panel with an inner diagonal cross. First of all, measure the door and mark out your panel and cross in pencil **(fig A)**.

A

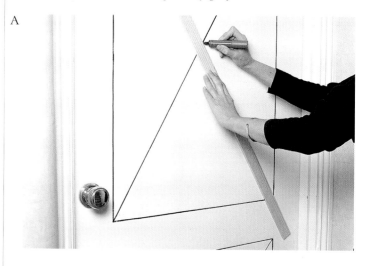

2 You will need to cut four pieces of moulding to make the frame, and one long diagonal piece and two short diagonal pieces for the inner cross. Once you have cut the lengths of moulding with the handsaw, you need to mitre the ends (see page 5). The long diagonal piece needs to be mitred on both sides of both ends. With each of the two short diagonal pieces, mitre the end that goes into the centre of the cross on one side at an angle of less than 45°. The ends of the short diagonal pieces that fit into the corners of the rectangle need to be mitred on both sides **(fig B)**.

3 Before sticking down the moulding, attach it with re-usable adhesive to make sure you have positioned it correctly. Once you are sure it all fits together, glue first the rectangular panel and then the inner cross in place **(fig C)**. Leave to dry for 24 hours.

B

C

4 If the pieces of moulding do not fit together quite perfectly (and they probably will not) fill up the cracks with a filler.

5 Once the glue and filler is dry, paint the moulding in the colour of your choice.

Painting Sisal Matting

Many of the decorative paint techniques used on floors and floor coverings in the past are still used today, adapted to make the most of modern materials. One of the simplest and most traditional ways of decorating a floor is to paint the floorboards, using either a plain colour on its own or with the addition of a stencilled design.

In the nineteenth century, it was usual to give a paint treatment only to the parts of floorboard that were not covered by carpet. A much more common sight, however, were decorative floorcloths made of canvas and painted with oil paints. In the eighteenth and nineteenth centuries they provided a cheap and colourful alternative to carpeting, and were particularly useful in areas of a house where valuable carpets would have been worn down too quickly. At first, floorcloths were hand-painted to imitate marbling, parquet and tiling; later, manufactured floorcloths became fashionable, until linoleum replaced them.

Painted mats

Today, when most furniture and household items are ready-made, anything individually crafted has a very special appeal. As an alternative to expensive, hand-painted floorcloths, you can paint your own sisal matting. Sisal is a modern product made from the leaves of the *Agave sisalana* plant. There is nothing new about using plant fibres for flooring – in early medieval times, rushes and straw were strewn on the floor, and, in summer, sweet-smelling herbs and flowers were added to give off a delicious scent as they were trodden down. Gradually, the rush or straw was woven into matting. Various types of matting continued to be used over the centuries, but in recent years it has become really fashionable. The superior quality of modern matting, and its lower cost compared to the equivalent in carpets, makes it very attractive. You can buy sisal matting in a wide variety of natural and dyed colours, and a range of hard-wearing weaves. As sisal matting takes oil paints particularly well, it offers considerable scope for the home decorator.

Decorating sisal matting is very simple – it can be stencilled or painted. For the beginner, bold geometric shapes are the easiest to attempt. Designs based on natural forms such as flowers and leaves are usually more difficult to apply, as curves are more complicated to produce than straight lines. Sisal floor covering can be used throughout the house, and it provides an excellent base for decorative rugs. Loose sisal mats are also available, and look best finished with a bound edge of jute border. In this project, a single sisal mat is stencilled with simple, but very effective, geometric shapes.

You will need:

- Sisal matting cut to the required size. We used a piece of sisal matting 1 x 1.2 metres (3 x 4 ft).
- Card
- Pencil
- Scissors
- Masking tape
- Stencil brush
- Red eggshell paint
- Green eggshell paint

Method

1 Work out the inner and outer border. According to the mat's dimensions, cut four strips of masking tape for the outer border and stick them 4 cm (1½ in) in from the edge of the mat. Then measure your inside border. In this example, it is 20 cm (8 in) in from the outer border. Stick a rectangle of masking tape 20 cm (8 in) from the outer border, then leave a gap of 2.5 cm (1 in) and stick another rectangle 23 cm (9 in) in from the outer border.

2 You can make the four-sided stars as large or small as you like. To draw a perfect four-sided star, draw a vertical line

A

and cross it with a horizontal line of equal length. Join up the four points of the cross to make a diamond shape. Measure the halfway point of each side of the diamond and draw a diagonal line through them. Mark the middle point of each of these four diagonal lines and draw lines from the halfway points to the tips of the original diamond shape. You will now have made a perfect four-sided star. Using this method, make one large star and six small stars.

B

C

MORE IDEAS

If you bind the edges of a sisal mat, you can add an extra touch by sticking studs along the binding.

3 Cut out the large star and place it in the middle of the inner rectangle. Outline the border of the star with masking tape. Place one small star in each of the four corners and one in the middle of the two long sides of the rectangle. Outline these in masking tape (**fig A**).

4 With a stencil brush, paint on the borders in red eggshell. Then paint the stars in green eggshell (**fig B**). Leave to dry for 4 to 6 hours and, when the paint is dry, peel off the masking tape.

5 To make the additional star points, measure halfway down the points of the cut-out stars you have already made and cut off the tips. Stick these tips between the green star points and outline them with masking tape. Stencil in with the red eggshell (**fig C**). Leave to dry for 4 to 6 hours.

Lino Cutting

Linoleum, or lino, is a durable floor-ing material invented by Frederick Walton, an Englishman, in 1863. Until the advent of petrol-based flooring products, lino had no equal, and its positive qualities have recently been rediscovered. Lino is made entirely from natural substances – a mixture of linseed oil, wood flour and pine resin, the last two being by-products of other industries. It is available in tiles and sheet form and comes in a wide range of colours (the attractive mar-bling is caused by the dyeing process itself). Being such a supple material, lino is easy to cut and inlay in almost any design. All-over geometrical patterns with straight edges are easiest to put down – curves are more tricky to cut and inlay accurately.

You will need:

➤ Red lino tiles

➤ Blue lino tiles

➤ Pencil

➤ Cardboard

➤ Scissors

➤ Stanley knife

➤ Linoleum tile adhesive

Method

1 First make the border. With a ruler measure a 5 cm (2 in) wide border along two sides of the blue tile, about 10 cm (4 in) in from the edge of the tile. Score along the ruler edge with the Stanley knife **(fig A)**. Then remove the two strips. Do the same on the red tile.

2 Draw a four-sided star on the card-board (see page 14). Cut out the star with the scissors. Place the template onto the centre of the red tile. Score

around it with the Stanley knife **(fig B)**. Remove the template and, using the Stanley knife, cut out the lino star. Repeat the process with the blue tile.

3 Place the red strips into the blue tile making a border.

4 Place the cut-out red star into the star shape in the blue tile **(fig C)**.

A

B

C

MORE IDEAS

Linoleum does not have to be confined to floors. It makes a warm and attractive surface for a desk or table top.

❖

Painting a Storage Chest in Tartan

Any type of plaid or check gives a bold and cheerful feel to a room, but the richest and most evocative of all plaids is tartan. An extremely versatile material, it adds warmth and colour to any room. You can be bold and use it extensively with a combination of tartan floor-length curtains together with a tartan carpet, set off by deep red-painted walls. Or you can use just a small amount of tartan to cover a couple of cushions or use it as upholstery material for a chair with just as stunning an effect. Alternatively, you can paint tartan as a design on a piece of furniture.

Tartan has a history, too. It conjures up images of Bonnie Prince Charlie in full Highland dress, of dark green hills splashed with purple heather and baronial stone halls hung with stags' heads. These images are far from fanciful. In the sixteenth and seventeenth centuries, tartan material was widely used to decorate Highland houses; it was hung on the walls for both decoration and warmth and draped over furniture. Lengths of it were worn as rough, belted kilts, with a trailing end which could be flung over the shoulder, leaving the sword arm free. In the eighteenth century, tartan became an important symbol of unity between Highland and Lowland Scots in their struggle against unification with England.

Today, there are over 700 registered tartans. These are of comparatively recent invention, and owe their existence to Queen Victoria in the late nineteenth century; her almost fanatical adoption of the material and thirst for creating new patterns probably secured its survival. She fell in love with Scotland and its traditions and ended up by carpeting and curtaining Balmoral (the royal residence in Scotland) in Royal Stewart. By doing so she instigated a fashion for using tartan in interior decoration.

In the early 1980s tartan was picked up by the designer Ralph Lauren, who promoted it as part of his up-market country look. Tartan has a kind of neutral quality that makes it easy to live with and means that it will blend happily with other colours in almost any decorating scheme. It can look really effective as a throw-over on the back of a sofa or made up into a tablecloth and edged with braid. Although 'modern' tartan has taken on a smartness in both dress and decoration, the material still evokes a strong link with heroic Scottish tradition.

You will need:

(For a medium-sized three-drawer chest)
- Tape measure
- Pencil
- Sandpaper
- 19 mm ($^3/_4$ in) masking tape
- 5 cm (2 in) wide and 6 mm ($^1/_4$ in) wide paintbrushes
- 1 lt (2 pt) tin of white wood primer
- 1 lt (2 pt) tin of dark grey undercoat (use white undercoat if you are painting a light-coloured tartan)
- 1 lt (2 pt) tin of raspberry-coloured, oil-based eggshell paint
- 0.5 lt (1 pt) tin of brownish-red, oil-based eggshell paint
- 0.5 lt (1 pt) tin of dark green, oil-based eggshell paint
- Steel wool
- White spirit for cleaning the brushes

Method

It is advisable to work in a well-ventilated room.

1 If you are using a chest of drawers which is already painted or has a varnish or wax finish, sand the chest down first using fine-grain sandpaper.

2 Remove the drawers, and paint the fronts of them and the outside frame with white wood primer. Leave to dry for 16 to 24 hours.

3 Paint over the primer with a coat of grey undercoat. Leave to dry for 6 to 16 hours.

4 Apply the background-colour paint (raspberry) to the drawer fronts and chest. You can use two coats of this if you wish, leaving each coat to dry for 16 to 24 hours.

5 When the background paint is completely dry, use a pencil and tape measure to mark out where the broad, 5 cm (2 in) horizontal stripes will be. Do this by finding the centre of each of the surfaces (sides, top, drawer fronts) and work outwards from there in 5 cm (2 in) sections. Leave a l0 cm (4 in) gap between each 5 cm (2 in) stripe. To make sure the lines stay straight and parallel, mark out a series of dots on the painted surface as a guide.

6 Using masking tape, which it is best to press on with a clean cloth rather than using your fingers, create a grid of horizontal stripes on the chest and drawer fronts.

7 Paint these stripes between the lengths of masking tape in the brownish-red colour, using the 5 cm (2 in) brush. Leave the stripes to dry for 16 to 24 hours, removing the masking tape after 4 hours (**fig A**).

8 When these first stripes are completely dry, repeat Stages 5 and 6, this time creating vertical 5 cm (2 in) stripes in the same brownish-red colour. Leave to dry for 16 to 24 hours, carefully removing the masking tape after 4 hours (**fig B**).

MORE IDEAS

You can easily create a scalloped effect on tartan ribbon by cutting round the shape of a coin with pinking shears.

❖

To hide the contents of open-fronted cupboards, make small curtains of tartan material.

❖

Tartan ribbon bows are an attractive alternative to hanging baubles on a Christmas tree.

❖

The word 'tartan' comes from the French 'tartaine', but the origins of the various designs are the subject of great controversy.

9 With a tape measure and pencil, mark out where the thin horizontal green stripes will go. These are 6 mm ($^1/_4$ in) thick, 2.5 cm (1 in) away from each side of the broad stripes.

10 With masking tape, create a grid for these thin lines, and using the 6 mm ($^1/_4$ in) brush, paint the green stripes between the lengths of masking tape **(fig C)**. Leave to dry for 16 to 24 hours, removing the masking tape after 4 hours.

11 Repeat Stages 9 and 10, this time to paint in the vertical, thin green stripes.

12 If your chest of drawers has wooden knobs, you can either paint in one of the plain colours or carefully continue the tartan pattern over them.

13 To give a final antique effect, gently brush a handful of fine, steel wool over the painted surface, which should be completely dry. This final technique will give a slightly worn or antique look to the wood.

Decorating a Shelf with Sheet Music

If you like the basic idea of découpage, but not the amount of work involved, use whole sheets of music or wrapping paper instead to cover furniture. A smart blue paper sprinkled with gold stars or dotted with shells and seaweed is ideal for a small bathroom cabinet. Old music sheets, torn up into long, even strips and pasted down in lines or quite higgeldy-piggeldy look striking on a small shelf unit or shelves.

You will need:

- ➤ Sheet music
- ➤ Access to a photocopier
- ➤ Wallpaper paste
- ➤ Paintbrush (for paste)
- ➤ Satin-finish varnish
- ➤ Brush for varnish

Method

1 If your shelf is rough, sand it before you start covering it.

2 Depending on the size of your shelf, photocopy the sheet music enough times to give you an all-over covering of paper.

3 Tear up the photocopies into a variety of shapes (**fig A**).

4 Mix up the wallpaper paste according to the manufacturer's instructions and, with a brush, carefully apply a layer of paste onto the backs of the torn photocopies. Stick them down, making sure as you do so that the pieces overlap with one another, so that every bit of the shelf will be covered (**fig B**). It is a good idea to wipe over the paper with a cloth once it is stuck down, pushing out any air bubbles that may be trapped under it.

5 Once the wallpaper paste is dry, varnish over the paper with a satin-finish varnish (**fig C**). Leave to dry for 6 hours.

MORE IDEAS

Take some pretty coloured gingham-patterned paper, fold it concertina-style and cut out the shape of a heart using a cardboard template. Use this to form a border around the top of a chest of drawers. Punctuate the drawers with individual heart shapes. You can also use the outlines of birds, animals and flowers in the same way.

❖

Autumn leaves make superb instant decorations. Collect fallen leaves and place them between sheets of newspaper under a pile of books to flatten and dry them off. Arrange and glue them onto your chosen piece, for example, as a border on a tray. Finish with a coat or two of varnish.

A

B

C

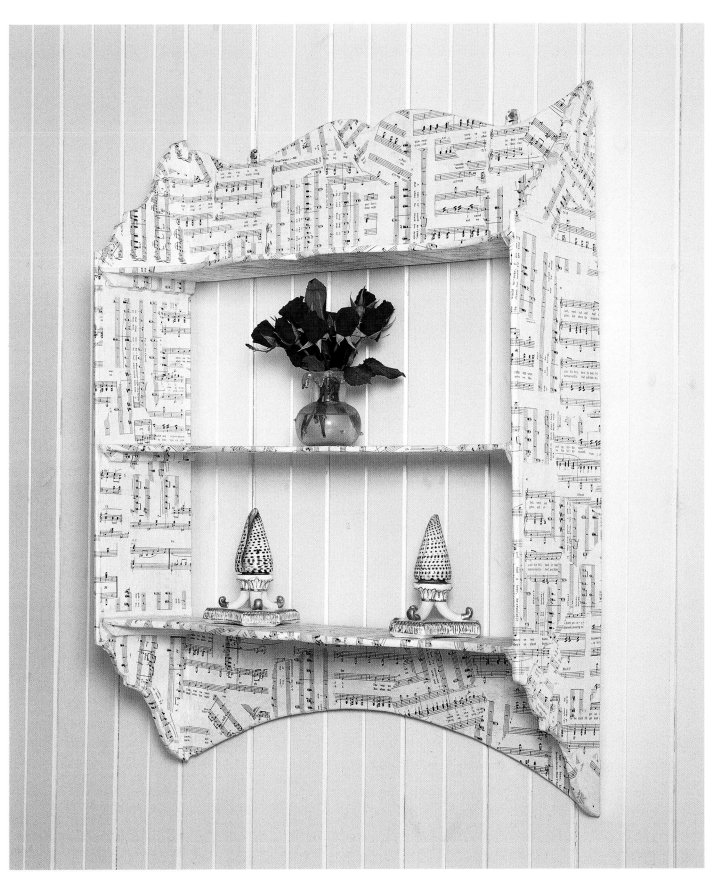

Stencilling a Wicker Basket

You will need:

- ➤ Wicker basket
- ➤ White undercoat paint
- ➤ White eggshell paint
- ➤ 5 cm (2 in) paintbrush
- ➤ Card
- ➤ Pencil
- ➤ Scissors
- ➤ Masking tape
- ➤ Blue emulsion paint
- ➤ Stencil brush (you can make your own by snipping off the end of an ordinary paintbrush to 2.5 cm (1 in)
- ➤ Varnish and brush

Method

1 Make the stencils by cutting the shape of the moon and stars out of card. You can draw these freehand or trace them from a book. Once you have drawn the outline, cut out the shape in the middle **(fig A)**, keeping the piece of card with the hollow image. This is your stencil.

2 Paint the basket in white undercoat and then, when dry, add a coat of white eggshell, leaving it to dry overnight.

3 Once the paint is dry, attach the stencils with masking tape in a design of your choice **(fig B)**.

4 Using the stencil brush, stencil on the blue emulsion in the cut-out images **(fig C)**. Apply the paint sparingly to the brush and dot inside the image lightly. In this way you will produce a textured effect. Leave to dry overnight.

A

B

MORE IDEAS

If you have some plain tiles in the bathroom or kitchen, it is possible to stencil them. Sand over the tiles with a rough sandpaper, dust, then prime with a universal adhesive and sealer. When the sealer has dried, brush on a topcoat of oil-based paint. The tiles are ready for stencilling using oil-based paints. To protect the decoration, varnish over the stencilled tiles.

❖

C

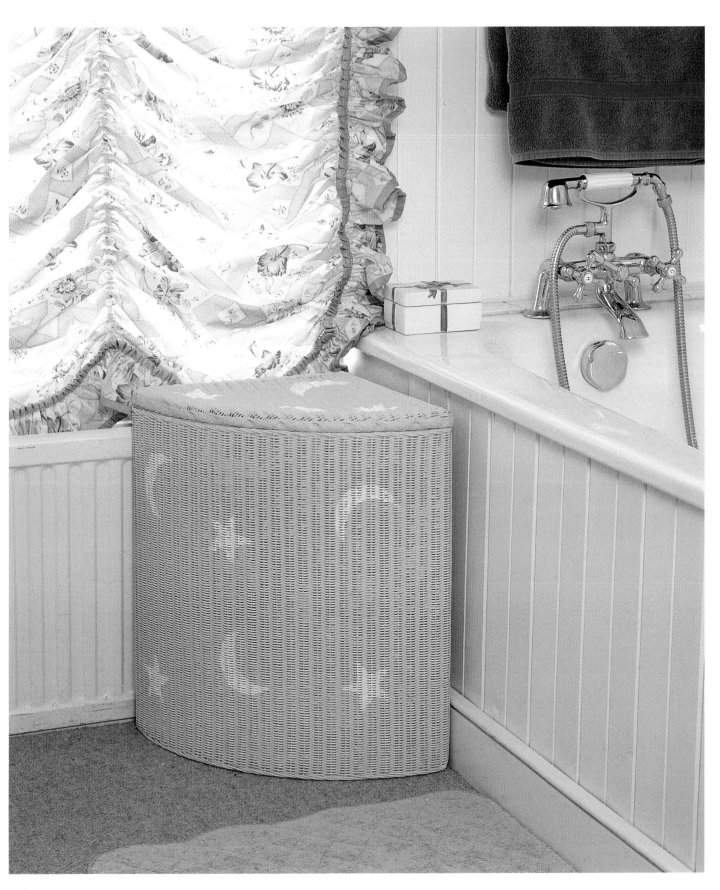

Upholstering a Drop-In Seat

With chairs and sofas, it is always worth buying the best quality you can and they will last you for life. It is also a good idea to make sure that the fabric you choose to cover your upholstered furniture is hard-wearing and will last. Until the nineteenth century, seating was for convenience rather than for comfort. Early attempts at upholstery were quite primitive and consisted simply of putting a pad, made of hair or fur, on top of a hard seat. Later, padding was attached to the bottom frame, which added some, but not much, comfort. In 1828, the invention of coil springs changed all this. By using them with the padding, furniture makers could produce upholstery which would both keep its shape and be infinitely more comfortable to sit on. They stuffed large and deeply sprung chairs and sofas almost to bursting point, covered them in plush materials, and used heavy buttoning for an even more sumptuous effect.

Today's hand-made upholstered furniture is expensive: it is made traditionally, using cotton wadding, felt, hogshair and natural fibres sprung over a solid beech frame. High-quality cushions are stuffed with duck down and feathers. In less expensive furniture, manufacturers substitute layers of foam for some of these materials. If there is too much foam, the seat will crumble away after a few years, necessitating re-upholstering. But upholstered dining chairs, in particular those with drop-in seats, are fortunately easy to change and can even be re-covered to suit a new colour scheme.

You will need:

- ➤ Plywood to fit over the frame of the chair seat
- ➤ Drill with 8 mm ($5/12$ in) bit
- ➤ Nails
- ➤ 1 metre (1 yard) covering material
- ➤ Staple gun and staples
- ➤ Stanley knife
- ➤ 1 metre (1 yard) of 4 cm- ($1^1/_2$ in-) thick foam
- ➤ 1 metre (1 yard) cotton wadding

Method

1 Dismantle the drop-in seat, including any webbing, and discard everything but the wooden frame (**fig A**).

2 Cut (or ask your wood merchant to cut) the plywood to the shape of the frame, but make sure it is 1 cm ($3/_8$ in) smaller all round. You can do this yourself if you make a template of the shape you need and saw the wood carefully so that there are no jagged edges.

3 Drill a few holes in the plywood using an 8 mm ($5/12$ in) bit. This will allow the upholstery to 'breathe'.

4 Fix the plywood to the frame with nails at 10 cm (4 in) intervals.

5 Put the frame on top of the foam, mark round it in pencil, and cut the foam along the lines with a Stanley knife so that you get a piece of foam 1.3 cm ($1/_2$ in) bigger than the frame. Lay the foam on top of the plywood.

6 Cut the cotton wadding to a size that is large enough to go over the foam with a little bit to spare.

7 Place the cotton wadding centrally over the foam, pull over the edges, and using the staple gun, attach it to the sides of the frame (**fig B**).

8 Cut to size the material you are using to cover the chair seat, making sure you have cut out enough material for Step 9.

9 Place the material centrally over the seat on top of the cotton wadding. Pull it firmly over the sides, folding it at the corners, and attach it to the underside of the frame with the staple gun (**fig C**).

A

B

**MORE
IDEAS**

*Before you buy a
piece of upholstered
furniture, test how
well it has been
made by taking out
the cushions and sit-
ting on the base. The
best sofas have a
sprung edge.*

❖

*Rather than buying
expensive furniture
from a department
store, it can be much
more rewarding to
look for chairs and
sofas in auction
rooms or junk shops.
Have them
professionally
restored or do it
yourself.*

❖

*Why not give a new
lease of life to an old
armchair or sofa,
without going to the
expense of re-covering
it? Instead, use a
throw-over such as a
shawl or rug.*

10 If you want a really professional
finish, cut a piece of hessian to
the size of the frame. Turn it in along
the edges, and staple it to the underside
of the seat, punching a hole in the
hessian where the dowel comes up from
the chair frame to anchor the drop-in
seat to the chair.

C

Stamping a Chair

Stamping or block printing was one of the earliest means by which fabrics were decorated mechanically. The method is simple: a relief image is carved onto a wooden block, dipped into ink, paint or dye, and then stamped onto a surface. By the eighteenth century many of the Indian calicoes or 'chints' (a type of earlty chintz), so sought-after in the West, were block printed in order to meet the huge export demand.

Block printing can be done with vegetables or fruit. Potatoes are a popular medium as they are easy to cut and offer a generous printing surface area, but carrots and turnips can also be used. Hard fruits, such as apples and pears, give a delicate print when they are halved. Remember to leave the cut area exposed to the air for a few minutes so that it goes brown – this dries out the surface and ensures a good print impression. You can also make an attractive print from ordinary household items such as string or rope. Glue lengths of them onto a wooden block to form an interesting pattern. When you print with them, you will produce a highly textured effect. You can use vegetable or wooden blocks to stamp a wide variety of items, including trays, boxes, furniture, wickerwork and fabric.

Stamping furniture

Before you start, test your stamps on paper first. This is vital, since no two stamps are alike, and you may need to make adjustments to the amount of pressure you apply in order to get a good result. Start with something simple, such as a mirror frame painted a plain colour in eggshell (eggshell offers a good base when it comes to stamping furniture). Place a stamp in the centre of each side, and one in each corner. Probably the easiest design would be flowers or leaves, or some form of geometric pattern. Instead of redecorating a whole room, you could just add a border. Or you could decorate the top of a chest of drawers with a border of stamped images, and perhaps the same stamped design on either side of the handle of each drawer. Chairs, chests, tables, boxes can all be treated in the same way. You can dust on an embossing powder, which comes complete with instructions, when working on furniture – it must be heated briefly (a hair dryer held at a safe distance is fine) to fix it. Always finish with an all-over coat of gloss or matt varnish to protect both the furniture and the stamped image.

You will need:

➤ Wooden chair
➤ 0.5 lt (1 pt) tin of eggshell paint
➤ Paintbrush
➤ Card
➤ Pencil
➤ Scissors
➤ Four potatoes cut into halves
➤ Kitchen knife or penknife
➤ Small tin of black poster paint
➤ Small tin of red poster paint
➤ Gloss or matt varnish

Method

1 Prepare the chair surface by cleaning it and painting it a plain colour in eggshell paint.

2 On the card, draw the stamp shapes: hearts, clubs, spades and diamonds. Carefully cut out the shapes. We have made large stamps for the chair seat and smaller ones for the frame.

3 Shape each potato half into a square. Place your card cut-out shape on top of the square surface and, with a sharp knife, cut around it (fig A). Remove the card and cut away under the shape at an angle so that you make a 'V' under your stamp. Leave the base of your block square – this is what you hold as you stamp. Make eight stamps; a large heart, diamond, spade and club, and a small set as well.

A

B

C

4 Once you have made your stamp shapes, you can start applying them to the chair. Dip each stamp into the poster paint and press it firmly onto the chair surface (**fig B**). Leave to dry for a couple of hours.

5 Once the paint is dry, apply a coat of varnish for protection (**fig C**). Leave to dry overnight.

Découpage Table Top

Découpage is the art of decorating surfaces with paper cut-outs and varnishing them to give the impression of hand-painting or inlay. Traditionally used on screens and boxes, it has vast decorative potential for almost any item and surface. Découpage became popular as an art around 1700, when it was first imported from China to Europe and was spread by merchants. A century later, reproductions were produced in Italy, where cabinet makers started using prints. It was sometimes known as *l'arte del uomo povero*, or 'poor man's art', which perfectly describes this inexpensive craft and its widespread application.

You can find good paper pictures and shapes in magazines, greetings cards, wrapping paper, and old catalogues such as seed catalogues. Some museum and craft shops may also sell modern copies of original cut-out print books or you can also hunt out old drawings and prints. If you copy these on a colour photocopier they will reproduce more realistically. Alternatively, cut out your own découpage pieces from coloured paper. Before you start, make a drawing of the object on paper and arrange the pieces until you are happy with the composition, then trace around the shapes as a guide. Make sure the surface you are sticking to is smooth and dust-free.

You will need:

- ➤ A glass-topped table
- ➤ Paper patterns or images to cut out. In this project, a piece of fabric has been photocopied.
- ➤ Scissors
- ➤ Glue for sticking glass. It must be a glue that dries absolutely clear.
- ➤ Paintbrush (for applying glue)
- ➤ Sheet of off-white paper
- ➤ Pencil

Method

1 Cut out the images carefully **(fig A)** and then arrange them on the glass.

2 Once you are happy with the arrangement, glue the pieces in position face up on the back of the glass using the paintbrush **(fig B)**. It is very important that you use clear-drying glue and that you apply it carefully, as you are applying the glue to the side of the cut-outs that will show beneath the glass, so any smudges will spoil the finished piece.

3 Once the images are glued on, take the piece of off-white paper and place the glass table-top over it. Draw around the outside edge with a pencil **(fig C)**. Cut around the pencil mark so that you end up with a piece of paper exactly the same size as the glass. Place the sheet of paper between the table and the glass top.

A

B

C

M O R E   I D E A S

You may like to stick to a specific theme when découpaging. You could consider cherubs and hearts, stars and moons, marine life, fruits and flowers, animals and birds, and the seasons.

Edging Shelves

It is easy to give shelving a new life using a range of inexpensive edgings and furnishing trims. In the nineteenth century, if you could not afford to finish off the shelves of your private library with turned mahogany mouldings (the shelves themselves would have been made of a much cheaper wood), you could choose to have less expensive smart leather edgings stuck on instead. These were made in deep, rich colours such as blues, reds, greens or black and had gilt embossed cutwork – often scallops or inverted triangles. You can still commission authentic edgings like this from specialist suppliers, but they are expensive and you would be better off using a ready-made moulding to edge your shelves.

The cheapest material to edge shelves with is paper. It is also the most flexible. Depending on the paper you choose – anything from wrapping paper to wallpaper – and the design you cut out, the edging can look architectural or lacy, plain or patterned, abstract or figurative. The easiest way to repeat a pattern is to fold the paper concertina-style, draw or trace on the image, then cut it out. Do not try to cut through too many layers of folded paper at once or you may run into trouble keeping clean-cut lines – it

is much better to cut out a series of lengths and then discreetly join them together at the back.

Ideas for designs of paper edgings range from the highly intricate to the simple. A geometric design such as a series of small diamonds within larger diamonds looks pretty and is simple to produce, whereas a figurative design such as a series of strutting cockerels is more difficult but very effective. Remember that the colour of the cut-out and the colour of the shelves will also contribute to the finished result. If you want an understated effect, go for a subtle combination, such as white on white, cream on cream or tones of the same colour – for example, a pale blue paper cut-out on shelves painted a slightly deeper blue. White shelves with pastel-coloured edgings look soft and pretty. The deeper and stronger the colour of the cut-out compared to that of the shelf, the bolder it will look.

If you want a really soft effect, use a furnishing trim. Open shelves or shelves in a bedroom cupboard would look attractive painted white, then edged with ribbon lace such as a broderie anglaise trim. Tartan ribbon would look very smart with shelves painted dark green or maroon to match.

You will need:

➤ Piece of fabric the length of your shelf and about 7.5 cm (3 in) deep

➤ Two bottle tops in different sizes

➤ Pinking shears

➤ Pencil

➤ Glue for sticking fabric to wood

Method

1 Place the template of your choice on the strip of fabric, close to one long edge, and draw around it, repeating as many times as necessary (**fig A**). We have used two alternating sizes of bottle top in our example.

2 Cut around the pencil lines with the pinking shears (**fig B**).

3 Glue the edging along the shelf (**fig C**).

A

B

MORE IDEAS

You could follow a particular theme when edging your shelves. For example, you could make a series of farm animals for the kitchen and choose a different geometrically patterned paper for each animal shape, such as stripes, ginghams and diagonals.

❖

Decorating Cupboard Doors

There are many ideas to choose from when it comes to cupboard doors. One of the most attractive is to replace the centre panel of each door with chicken-wire and hardboard, as shown in this project. An undistinguished cupboard is instantly smartened up, and if the panels are already in poor condition, this may be a cheaper solution than replacing the doors.

Many smaller side cupboards, known as chiffoniers, were constructed along these lines in the eighteenth and nineteenth centuries. Instead of chicken wire, they had brass grilles for panels, and these were sometimes backed with silk gathered into pleats. Glass was expensive in the eighteenth century, so insetting the doors with grilles was probably an economy measure. Chiffonier fronts are now more commonly found covering boxed-in radiators – one way of disguising a very necessary twentieth-century innovation. You may, of course, use brass wire for door panels, but chicken-wire looks just as smart. You can either leave the wire absolutely plain or paint it using an oil-based paint (prime it with a metal primer first). Choose whether or not to add the hardboard backing – some clothes cupboards in English country houses used chicken-wire alone, and to great effect. A gathered fabric backing looks stylish: simply gather and pin the fabric to the back of the door, or sew a narrow casing at top and bottom and thread plastic-covered spring wire through, neatly gathering the fabric as you work along. Hook the ends of each spring wire to rings fixed inside either side of the door panel.

Fabric can be used in this way to back functional glass-fronted cupboards. If you add hardboard backing, you can paint the panels a plain colour or apply a special paint effect such as dragging or sponging. Alternatively, stick on a decorative paper – wrapping paper is ideal as it is cheap, and comes in a wide range of designs, as does wallpaper. *Trompe-l'oeil* papers are very effective, particularly those with false books or crockery on them.

You will need:

- Tape measure
- Hardboard, cut to size
- Pencil
- Scissors
- Wallpaper or wrapping paper
- Chicken wire
- Wire cutters
- Staple gun
- Glue
- Nails or some other device for attaching panels to cupboard

Method

1 Measure the panels on your exisiting cupboard and buy hardboard panels to fit.

2 Lay a hardboard panel on top of the wallpaper or wrapping paper, draw around it with a pencil and cut out as many pieces of paper as you need (fig A). Glue the paper panels to the hardboard panels (fig B).

3 Using the wire cutters, cut the chicken wire 7.5 cm (3 in) larger all round than the hardboard panels.

4 Lay a piece of chicken wire over a hardboard panel and bend the edge of the wire around the panel, stapling to the board (fig C). Repeat this for each of the panels. To fix the panels to the door, use nails or brackets. Ask at a DIY store for advice.

A

B

MORE IDEAS

*An arrangement of shells looks
striking stuck onto a cupboard
door. You could stick on a
narrow border of shells around the
edges. In the centre you could put a
single motif, such as a starfish.*

❖

*Découpage (see pages 22 and 28)
is an excellent way of decorating
cupboard doors. In a child's room,
you could use a theme such as
'the jungle' or 'the farmyard'.*

Solving Storage Problems

Storage is often a problem. In particular, it is hard to know where to store things in a neat and attractive way. Here are some suggestions that are both practical and decorative.

A screen is useful for blocking out unattractive storage boxes with no place to go. Cover the screen with fabric or paint, or découpage it (see pages 28–29). You can make your own screen out of three rectangular wooden frames (preferably hardboard) held together by a series of hinges, and with a cheap fabric, such as calico, stretched over. This part of the operation is made easier if you use a staple gun, otherwise use small nails to hold the fabric in place at the back of the frames. If you want to prepare the screen for découpage, prime the calico with an acrylic primer or a thinned coat of emulsion, then brush on one or two coats of emulsion to give it a smooth surface on which to work. Stretch elastic or ribbon across to form a trellis in which to insert and store notes, letters and cards as shown in the project.

A chest or trunk is an invaluable storage item and one of the few pieces of furniture no medieval household of any standing would be without. By the fifteenth century, a wealthy bride always brought a magnificent wedding chest (known as a *cassoni*) to her new home; it was often sumptuously carved and painted with pastoral scenes. But the dowry chests that will probably inspire you to get out your paints are those decorated by the Pennsylvanian Germans in America. These were hand-painted with traditional folk art motifs, such as as mermaids, unicorns, griffins, or the tree-of-life and hearts, and had plain or combed backgrounds. A combed effect on its own looks good on a wooden or tin trunk.

Decorating a Trunk

You will need:

- Tin trunk
- 1 lt (2 pt) tin of grey undercoat
- 1 lt (2 pt) tin of green eggshell paint
- Paintbrush
- Old credit card
- Scissors
- 1 lt (2 pt) tin of black eggshell paint

Method

1 Paint the trunk in grey undercoat. Leave to dry overnight.

2 Paint over the trunk with the green eggshell. Leave to dry overnight (**fig A**).

3 With the scissors, cut a serrated edge along the credit card to make a comb.

4 Paint over the green paint with the black eggshell (**fig B**). Quickly, before it dries, drag the comb down over the green paint, creating a wavy line effect (**fig C**). Leave to dry for 16 hours.

A

B

C

Screen with Ribbons

You will need:

- Screen
- Length of ribbon, 2.5 cm (1 in) wide
- Scissors
- Staples and staple gun
- Needle and thread

Method

1 Measure each panel of the screen and divide it into four sections with a pencil line. Each of these sections will have a diagonal cross of ribbon. Work out how much ribbon you require to create the criss-cross effect. Cut out eight lengths of ribbon.

2 Start at the top of the screen. Hold one piece of the ribbon to one corner, tuck 1 cm (3/8 in) of ribbon over the corner and staple it down. Pull the other end of the ribbon diagonally across a quarter of the screen, keeping it taut. Tuck 1 cm (3/8 in) of ribbon behind the screen and staple it down. Repeat this over the four sections of the screen.
Then repeat from the other side to create the cross.

3 With the needle and thread, sew a couple of stitches in the centre of each cross, attaching it to the screen.

Racing-Car Bedhead

The ideal child's room is both practical and fun. Essentially, this means that whatever decorative elements you introduce, choose surfaces that can be easily cleaned and fabrics that are hardwearing. Always make sure that there is plenty of space for storing toys and clothes.

When choosing wallpaper, it is worth noting that while pictorial designs are excellent for stimulating a small child's interest, older boys will probably prefer a simple check or stripe. If you decide on paint, don't cover all the walls in a dark colour as this may prove claustrophobic. Many children will treat their walls with little respect, seeing them as a convenient noticeboard for their posters and photographs, so it may be a good idea to provide a real noticeboard to minimize the damage!

Painted furniture is an excellent idea for a child's room. Tables, chairs, bookcases or a chest of drawers can be painted with a design of their choosing. It can always be repainted as the child grows up. When deciding on a bed, although they may be more expensive, bunk beds are extremely useful when friends stay overnight; they are also space saving and, of course, fun. If you choose a single bed, you can create a specialized bedhead, such as the one in this project.

You will need:

- Plain wooden bedhead
- Fine sandpaper
- Soapy warm water and cloth
- Small tin of grey undercoat
- Small tin of matt black eggshell paint
- Medium-sized paintbrush
- 4 metres (4 yards) of 7.5 cm- (3 in-) wide black-and-white check ribbon or paper border
- Colour pictures of cars from posters or glossy motoring magazines. It is important that the paper is thick rather than flimsy, as the latter is difficult to glue and will tear easily.
- Scissors
- Re-usable adhesive
- Wallpaper glue and fabric glue (if you are using ribbon)
- Small tin of clear satin varnish

Method

1 Sand the bedhead down to remove all varnish and create a smooth surface.

2 Wash the surface lightly with warm soapy water. Wipe it clean and leave until the wood is completely dry.

3 Using a medium-sized paintbrush, apply a coat of grey undercoat to the bedhead. Leave it to dry for 12 to 16 hours.

4 With the same brush paint the bedhead all over, including the sides, with matt black eggshell. Leave to dry for 24 hours.

5 Cut the ribbon or paper border into four lengths, two long and two short, to fit along the sides of the bedhead exactly. If the width of your border is much less than 7.5 cm (3 in), you will need a double width to create the right effect (**fig A**).

6 Carefully and thoroughly apply the glue to the surface of the border, and stick the lengths one at a time round the edges of the bedhead, overlapping them at each corner.

A

B

7 Cut out the cars carefully (**fig B**). Decide on the arrangement you are going to have for the cut-out cars. You can use
one big one, lots of little ones, or a combination of the two. Make
sure that your design will fit in the space within the border before
you start sticking the cars to the bedhead.

8 Attach the cut-out cars to the bedhead with the re-usable
adhesive. Once you are sure they are positioned correctly,
stick them on with the wallpaper glue, making sure you cover the
backs of the cut-out cars all over. Firmly press the cars onto the
bedhead, smoothing each one out so there are no air bubbles or
creases (**fig C**). Leave for 24 hours so that the glue has plenty of
time to harden.

9 Finally, with the medium-sized paintbrush, apply a coat of
clear satin varnish over the cars and the sides of the bedhead,
but not over the ribbon. Leave for a further 12 hours, or until the
varnish is completely dry.

C

Gingham Ribbon Bedspread

Most girls have definite ideas on how they want their room to look and the majority, though not all, will want the final effect to be pretty and feminine, probably with pastel colours and lots of attractive details. Curtains can bring an element of colour and pattern into a room; however, very bright or heavy designs may dominate it. Pretty lined or unlined voile curtains always look good, as do simple gingham blinds with a frill around the edges.

Young girls have masses of toys which, as they grow older, turn into piles of clothes. So when you are planning furniture, be sure to buy a large enough wardrobe. You can paint it in a soft colour to match the room, then stencil on bunches of flowers.

Alternatively, instead of a wardrobe, you can hang a rail with a curtain across a corner of the room.

For younger girls, leave a corner of the room clear so that they can create a 'home' area where they can have tea parties with dolls, play games with friends, or make a toy shop. For older girls, if the room is large enough, find an old sofa which you can cover with a throw-over. It will be a great place for your child to curl up and read her books. A towel with her name sewn on it, a hairbrush with a hand-painted back or a colourful fabric coat-hanger will all be treasured, and a pretty bedspread, which you can either buy or make yourself, may even encourage her to make her bed.

You will need:

- Calico material large enough to cover the bed with overhang at the sides and bottom. (If one piece is not wide enough, sew together two pieces of calico, using plain flat seams.)
- Tape measure
- Soft pencil
- Pins
- Strong pale cream sewing thread
- Sewing machine
- Quantity of pink gingham ribbon 5cm (2 in) wide. The amount you need will depend on both the size of the bed-spread and the squares. As a guide, for a 1.8x2.4 metres (6x8 ft) bedspread you will need 21 metres (21 yards) of ribbon if you are going to sew 60 cm (2 ft) squares, and 37 metres (37 yards) if you decide on 30 cm (1 ft) squares.
- Piece of lining material 2.5 cm (1 in) larger all round than the calico

Method

1 Knowing the dimensions of the material, first work out on paper what size your squares of ribbon are going to be. You should take into account the fact that the smaller the squares, the more ribbon you will need, and also that you will be using a border of ribbon all round the bedspread edges.

2 Lay the calico material flat on the floor, and with the help of a tape measure transfer the grid system you have worked out on paper onto the material, drawing the lines faintly with a soft pencil (**fig A**).

3 Cut as many strips of ribbon as you need to go on the bed-spread lengthwise, and pin them to the calico along the marked-out lines.

4 Cut as many strips of ribbon as you need to go across the width of the bedspread. Weave these alternately over and under the long strips, as if you were darning, and pin them to the calico (**fig B**).

A

B

5 When the pattern of squares is complete, sew the ribbon to the calico by machine (**fig C**). Machine on the border at the same time as sewing on the lining. The calico should overlap the lining by 2.5 cm (1 in) all round.

MORE IDEAS

❖

*Make two tails from a material of your choice to represent the
trailing ribbons of a bow. Sew them together to form an inverted
'V' shape, then staple them to a wall. Make a bow out of the same
material and attach this to the wall so that it covers the staples.*

❖

*To contain the clutter of hair slides and jewellery, invest
in a small wicker basket, which you can decorate with ribbons
and bows.*

❖

*Use any left-over ribbon to trim small plain white cushions
to place on the bed during the day.*

Painting a Cache-Pot

The decorative art of painting on metal is known as tole. The word 'tole' is French for sheet iron, and it was from sheet iron that the earliest examples of decorated metalware were made. This dates back to seventeenth-century Europe, when trade with the Far East was flourishing and for the first time Europeans came into contact with imported Japanese and Chinese objects, beautifully decorated with ornamental lacquerwork. They were an immediate success, and demand soon outweighed supply. As the pieces were extremely expensive, European craftsmen began to copy the techniques and style of oriental lacquerwork onto metal household objects, using a process whereby paint could be applied to tin.

The metal is moulded into attractive shapes, sometimes with pierced or scalloped edges, giving toleware a delicate appearance. It comes in a wonderful variety of colours, from dark greens, red and blues to creams and pastels, beautifully decorated and with a rich, effective use of gold paint either in the applied design or as a contrast round the rim.

This painted tinware became fashionable for items such as tea, coffee and chocolate tins. In the late seventeenth century, most coffee houses stored their beverages in painted tinware boxes which were hygienic, cheap, practical and, above all, attractive to look at. They would brighten up an interior in a way that earthenware pots could not do.

Like many fashions, tole eventually lost its popularity and there is now very little around. Antique tole items are highly collectable and can be worth almost as much as the lacquerwork they originally copied. Not surprisingly, tole has now become fashionable again and it is possible that modern pieces of hand-painted reproduction tole, made using traditional methods and designs, could be the valuable antiques of the future. However, for the present, just one or two of these attractive reproductions, such as a wastepaper basket or wall sconce, can make all the difference to the look of a room. One of the most popular uses of tole is for cache-pots, the French name for plant holders.

You will need:

- Plain metal cache-pot/planter – preferably with a decorative rim
- Small tin of light grey metal primer (substitute white primer if you want to use pale colours)
- Small tin of dark red eggshell paint
- Small tin of dark green eggshell paint
- Quantity of stick-on paper stars (depending on the number of stars you want in your decoration)
- l9 mm (³/4 in) masking tape.
- Good quality 5 cm (2 in) paintbrush
- White spirit for cleaning brushes
- Clean soft cloth

Method

1 Using the 5 cm (2 in) brush, paint the outside of the cache-pot with metal primer. Leave it to dry for at least l6 hours.

2 Using the same brush, cover the primer with a coat of dark red eggshell paint (fig A). You can use two coats of this if you wish, leaving each coat to dry for l6 to 24 hours.

3 When the red paint is completely dry, attach vertical strips of masking tape at regular 5 cm (2 in) intervals round the outside of the cache-pot over the red paint. Decorate the spaces in between these strips with stick-on stars. After you stick on the masking tape and stars wipe over the edges with a clean cloth, to make sure they are completely stuck down. This will prevent any seepage when the next layer of paint is applied.

A

4 When you have checked that the strips and stars are firmly attached, carefully apply the green eggshell paint all over the cache-pot. You don't have to paint over all the masking tape as long as you make sure the edges are covered with green, but it is a good idea to paint over the stars so that you get a clear definition of their shape (fig B). Leave to dry for 24 hours.

5 Carefully peel off the masking tape and stars to reveal the red pattern underneath (fig C).

C

MORE IDEAS

Instead of using a cache-pot, decorate a watering can. This looks very attractive standing on the floor. For extra effect, paint the star shapes and sprinkler head in gold.

Shell Mirror

Beachcombing for shells is one of life's simpler pleasures. Walking along the sand at low tide, you can find a wide variety of collectable shells. Once home, however, what do you do with them? In the eighteenth and nineteenth centuries, they would have been displayed in collectors' cabinets, used to decorate walls and ceilings to form a grotto, made into pictures, and used to adorn frames or boxes. Collectors' cabinets are an expensive item these days, but an equally attractive way to display your finest shell specimens on the wall is in a shadow box lined with fabric, preferably one that has a clip-on glass front to keep off the dust.

You could alternatively make a 'Sailor's Valentine'. These were popular in the nineteenth century and consisted of an open container divided into compartments in which shells were laid out in patterns with a central motif, such as a heart, in each compartment. The heart was usually made up of small overlapping shells surrounded by a wide, circular border of shells. The circle was divided into segments, each one containing a different species of shell laid out in horizontal or vertical rows. You can make a 'Sailor's Valentine' with, for example, a hexagonally-sided chocolate box. Cover it with a suitable paper or fabric and then glue in the shells.

Shells are a perfect medium for mosaic work. The Romans created mosaics on fountains and the walls of grottoes. These features were later taken up by the Renaissance Italians. From Italy, the fashion for extravagant grottoes complete with fabulous shell designs, petrifications, crystals and rockwork spread to France and England and later to Germany. Grotto shellwork in particular was a source of inspiration for the exuberant Rococo style that dominated interior design during the eighteenth century in Europe. In the shell pavilion at Goodwood Park, Sussex, in England, the Duchess of Richmond and her two daughters took seven years to decorate every bit of the interior with shells.

A shell mosaic on a piece of hardboard makes a fine decorative panel for a wall. Indeed, any flat surface is suitable for this treatment, for example, doors, cabinets, chests, or even a side table. Whatever the scale of the project, take time planning your design and do not be too ambitious. For inspiration and ideas look at examples of past shell work. You will discover, as ever, that the most successful schemes are also usually the simplest.

You will need:

➤ Framed mirror
➤ Selection of shells
➤ Glue (special glue, obtainable from a craft shop)
➤ Varnish

Method

1 Wash the mirror frame with soap and water. Dry it well.

2 Plan your shell pattern by laying out the shells around the outside of the frame or by drawing a design beforehand (**fig A**).

3 If your frame already has a mirror in it, cover the mirror glass with newspaper to protect it.

4 Cover the frame with glue and stick on your shells carefully following the pre-planned design. It is a good idea to stick on the large shells first (**fig B**).

5 Varnish the shells for protection (**fig C**).

A

B

MORE IDEAS

Stick shells on boxes and photograph frames.

❖

Transform old flowerpots by covering them with shells.

Papier Mâché Bowl

Papier mâché is a simple, tough and wonderfully versatile medium. In the eighteenth and nineteenth centuries, manufacturers produced a wide variety of papier mâché goods ranging from trays and boxes to furniture and architectural ornamental features, such as ceiling roses and panelling. The decorative possibilities are even wider. Traditional papier mâché treatments encompass everything from the lacquerwork so popular in the nineteenth century, which drew on Chinese motifs for its inspiration (see pages 52–53), to the exuberant designs and colours of folk-art artefacts from Mexico and India.

The technique – applying strips of pasted paper or paper pulp to a form or mould – has not changed since the Chinese discovered how to make paper in about 200 AD, and then found a way to recycle valuable scraps. This new product proved to be so light, yet tough, that it was used by the Chinese to make their war helmets; these same properties make it ideal for creating trays, bowls, plates and frames.

One of the easiest ways to get started with papier mâché is to use it to rejuvenate an old, scratched tray, table or mirror or picture frame. Once the surface has been covered with papier mâché, it can be decorated. If you prefer to create a new object, a surprising number of everyday items can be used for moulds: pudding basins, bowls, baking tins, trays, baskets and plates are just some of the possibilities.

Decorative options

Now to the fun part – the decoration. If you are unsure of your artistic ability, a simple but effective finish is to stick layers of tissue paper over a plain base colour, finishing with a coat of varnish or lacquer to protect the surface. Sticking on paper cut-outs also works well. If you want to produce a floral design on your finished papier mâché, wrapping paper is a good source of images. Paint techniques, such as ragging, sponging, combing and spattering require little skill but are impressive. Or you can try reliefwork on decorative objects by sticking on string, rope, cardboard cut-outs, or shells and stones, then painting them.

If you want to create your own design, work it out on paper first and then transfer it to the papier mâché form using tracing paper. You will find inspiration in wallpaper and fabric patterns or books on crafts and the decorative arts. To begin, try making something simple, such as this papier mâché bowl.

You will need:

- One black-and-white newspaper
- One coloured paper newspaper
- 0.5 lt (1 pt) wallpaper paste
- One balloon
- Mixing bowl
- Washing-up liquid
- 2.5 cm (1 in) paintbrush
- Pencil
- Scissors
- Small tin of white undercoat paint
- Small tin of dark blue gloss paint
- Small tin of gold paint
- Gold paper stars
- Gloss varnish
- Three dark blue beads

Method

1 Tear about half of the black-and-white and half of the coloured newspapers into approximately 5 cm (2 in) squares.

2 Mix up the wallpaper paste according to the packet instructions.

3 Blow up the balloon. Place it in a bowl or saucepan, and cover it with a layer of washing-up liquid.

4 Apply the first layer of newspaper over the balloon, then add the paste with the paintbrush and then the next layer of paper **(fig A)**. The point of using different coloured paper is so that you can tell which layer is which. Eight layers in all are required. Do not try to get an even surface – it is impossible to achieve this with papier mâché. Leave it to dry for about 3 to 4 days in a room where the temperature is steady. This should prevent the balloon from sinking.

5 Burst the balloon with a pin. Place over the papier mâché a bowl of similar size to the one you want to make and draw around the top edge with a pencil. Then remove the bowl and cut around the pencil marking with scissors **(fig B)**.

A

6 To produce a smooth edge, cover the rim with a couple of layers of papier mâché.

7 Apply three coats of white undercoat to the surface with a 2.5 cm (1 in) paintbrush. Allow the paint to dry between each coat. Then paint on a coat of dark blue gloss paint (fig C).

8 To decorate the bowl, paint a thin line of gold paint around the inner and outer rim. Stick some gold paper stars onto the outer surface of the bowl. Apply two coats of varnish to all surfaces and leave to dry for overnight.

9 Stick three beads in a triangle to the bottom of the bowl – they will help it to sit properly. You can either buy the beads in the appropriate colour or you can paint them yourself.

MORE IDEAS

If you are using fruit or vegetables as moulds, you will need to cover the mould with vaseline so that once the papier mâché is set you can remove it easily. You will then have to apply another couple of layers of papier mâché so that you can paint the finished item.

Lampshades

There are various methods you can use to decorate plain modern fabric or card lampshades. In the nineteenth century, lampshades were made of fabric trimmed with gathered silk or lace, or hung with fringes around the base. If you like this look, you can add a broderie anglaise or lace trim to a plain fabric lampshade or use a piece of lace to cover the whole shade. Tuck a very small hem of lace over the top of the shade and glue it in place. It looks pretty if you allow the lace to fall below the bottom edge of the shade. Alternatively, you can cover a bare strutted frame with lace lined in a plain fabric, which has been gathered with ribbon at the top and bottom. Secure the covering to the frame by sewing the inner lining fabric to the top and bottom rings.

By the 1920s, lampshades made of parchment or vellum were very popular. These were often hand-painted with landscapes or seascapes, or had a scenic print stuck centrally to the front of the shade. Modern card and card-backed fabric lampshades can be treated in the same way, using either acrylic or oil-based paints. As the project on the right shows, animal-skin markings are easy to simulate – you could also try tiger stripes or leopard spots. Alternatively, ready-cut clear acetate stencils are flexible enough to be used on the curve of a lampshade, and there are plenty of good designs around to choose from. An even easier option is to stick cutouts onto the shade. This could be either a print or images taken from wrapping paper or wallpaper (remember that you can always increase or decrease the size of the image on a black-and-white or colour photocopier).

Another easy way to transform a lampshade is to introduce some form of trimming at the top and bottom of the shade, such as a braid, rope or fringe. This can either match the colour of the shade or you can use it to provide contrast. For example, if your colour scheme is predominantly pale blue and you have chosen an off-white shade, a complementary pale blue trim will provide a good contrast.

Zebra-Stripes Lampshade

You will need:

- ➤ Plain fabric lampshade
- ➤ Picture of a zebra
- ➤ Pencil
- ➤ Small pot of black fabric paint
- ➤ Artist's brush, no 6

Method

1 Look through nature books or magazines for a picture of a zebra. Ideally, copy the zebra stripes free-hand. Alternatively, using the pencil, draw a box over one area of the zebra picture.

2 Again using the pencil, copy the section of zebra markings that you have highlighted onto the lampshade so that it makes an attractive pattern.

3 With the artist's brush, paint over your pencil drawing with the black fabric paint. Leave to dry overnight.

Pleated Lampshade

You will need:

- Sheet of thick paper (but thin enough to allow light to shine through), plain, coloured or patterned, such as wrapping paper
- Tape measure
- Wallpaper border (optional)
- String
- Hole punch
- Ribbon
- Paper glue

Method

1 Measure the height and circumference of a lampshade (the same size as the one you want to make) and cut the piece of thick paper to the same height and double the width. If you have chosen plain paper, stick on a wallpaper border for decorative effect.

2 Measure your first paper pleat of 1 cm (3/8 in) with the tape measure. Use this first pleat as a guide for the other pleats. Once you have pleated the whole sheet of paper, score down each pleat with scissors to make the folds crisp. With all the pleats folded, tie up

the paper with string at both ends and in the middle, to ensure the pleats stay in.

3 With the shade still tied up, using the hole punch, make a hole that runs through all the pleats, 4 cm (1½ in) from the top end of the shade.

4 Untie the paper and, on the reverse side, punch holes in the crease of each fold 1 cm (3/8 in) from the top end. (These holes will form a ridge that will rest on the lampstand and keep the lampshade stable.)

Ribbon Lampshade

You will need:

- Plain fabric lampshade
- Gingham ribbon, 2 cm (3/4 in) and 4 cm (1½ in) wide
- Tape measure
- Scissors
- Fabric glue

Method

1 Measure the height of the lampshade and add 6 cm (2½ in) to allow for turning over the ends and sticking them down. Cut the 4 cm- (1½ in-) wide gingham ribbon into strips. To work out how many strips you need, measure the top circumference of the lampshade and divide by the width of the ribbon. Using fabric glue, stick the ribbon in straight lines from the top to the bottom of the

lampshade, leaving about 3 cm (1¼ in) at both ends, which you turn over and stick down.

2 Cut the 2 cm- (3/4 in-) wide gingham ribbon into strips, tie the strips into bows and stick onto the lampshade.

Plasterwork

Plasterwork in the form of ceiling roses, cornices and mouldings is a marvellous way to add interest to a room. Even a simple cornice helps to define and soften the line where wall meets ceiling, and restoring the curves of a ceiling rose will provide a focal point in an expanse of ceiling.

Many of the motifs that appear in the cornices and centrepieces available today date back to the Romans, who were the first to use decorative stucco work in interiors. They drew widely from nature, mythology and legends for their motifs, which included flower garlands and wreaths and figures of heroes, goddesses and centaurs. These were all modelled in low-relief stucco and framed by mouldings such as beading and trellis designs.

Modelled relief-work

Plasterwork was widely used throughout Europe, and later in America, from the seventeenth century onwards, not only for features such as centrepieces, cornices and mouldings but also to provide high-relief frames for pictures and mirrors. You can create similar decorative features, using modelling clay instead of plaster and mouldings. Make flowers and leaves into the shape of a wreath to decorate the front of a plain fireplace, or form them into swags or festoons to run across the fireplace and down each side. Doors and cupboard fronts can be embellished by adding plasterwork panels of different sizes in the form of ready-made mouldings (see pages 12–13).

Foliage is easy to model as leaves themselves can be pressed into the clay to form the shape, as shown in the following project. Flowers are too fragile for this process, but fortunately many flower shapes are easy to model. Wild roses, daisies and pansies all have simple yet distinctive outlines. You can find the patterns in an illustrated gardening book or, perhaps surprisingly, in any good cake-decorating manual. Pastry cutters are useful for a serrated edge, and you may find some suitable pastry shapes, such as stars, that can be incorporated into your design. If you want to repeat a floral motif several times, make a template out of cardboard and trace round it with a knife on the rolled-out clay. For a more realistic appearance, lightly trace lines in the clay flowers to suggest veining on petals, and use a sharp pencil point to dot in the stamens. While the baked clay is still cooling, gently manipulate the petals to curve up or back slightly to make them look more life-like.

Clay Modelling on Frames

You will need:

- Plain wooden frame
- Small packet of modelling material (you can buy this at most art and craft shops)
- Leaves
- Sharp kitchen knife
- Small tin of white undercoat paint
- Baking tray
- Glue for sticking clay to wood
- Small tin of eggshell paint (we used yellow)

Method

1 If you are using an old frame, prepare it first by giving it a coat of white undercoat.

2 Roll out the modelling clay to approximately 3 mm (1/8 in) thick.

3 Lay a leaf onto the rolled-out clay and press down, leaving an impression of the leaf and its veins on the clay. Cut around the leaf impression with a sharp kitchen knife (**fig A**).

A

4 Place the cut-out shapes onto a baking tray. Follow the manufacturer's instructions regarding the temperature and the length of time you should bake the clay. We baked our clay for 15–20 minutes at 130°C (275°F). The leaves can be slightly bent when they are cooling in the tray.

B

5 Once the leaf shapes are baked, stick them onto the frame with the glue in a design of your choice (**fig B**). The clay we used took about 1 hour to harden, so, if necessary, you can reshape a piece at this stage.

6 Once the the leaves are stuck down, paint them in the colour of your choice with eggshell paint (**fig C**).

C

MORE IDEAS

Use ready-made wooden beading to create a 'stucco work' frieze. Decide on the width of the frieze and then work out how much extra beading you need for each vertical to create evenly-spaced rectangular compartments. Prepare and paint the beading before carefully gluing it to the wall. Paint the wall area within the frieze darker or lighter than the beading.

Silhouettes

Silhouettes have captivated and intrigued people ever since prehistoric man daubed the walls of caves with the outlines of sacred animals. That these powerful images are instantly recognizable to us thousands of years later is proof both of the skill of those early artists and the wonderful immediacy of profile art. Civilization after civilization reinterpreted the silhouette – notably the Egyptians, Etruscans and Greeks – but it was only in the eighteenth and nineteenth centuries that they flourished as a popular form of portraiture. Before the photograph, the silhouette was the only easy and accessible method of achieving likenesses by amateur and professional artists, and provided inexpensive decorations.

If you like elegant images from the past and cannot afford originals, you can always copy old silhouettes to hang on your walls. Creating silhouettes of your own family and friends, however, is much more entertaining and personal. Seat your subject in front a bright light and trace the shadow onto a white sheet of paper pinned to a board placed in the correct position. You can leave the profile full size or reduce it down, and then paint it in with black paint. In nineteenth-century America, two very popular silhouette methods were to cut the image out in black paper or to cut out an image and place the hollowed-out piece of paper against a background. The basic outline was achieved as already described, although some silhouette artists were so skilled with a pair of scissors that they could snip out an accurate likeness freehand in only three minutes. Hollow-cut silhouettes look very pretty placed on a wallpaper or fabric background – silk, satin or velvet are all authentic for the eighteenth and nineteenth centuries.

Personalized silhouettes

Apart from bust and full-length vignettes, conversation pieces depicting family and friends engaged in various leisure activities were also fashionable in the nineteenth century. Some of the most charming examples are of children either at play or posing with a favourite pet. These were painted or cut freehand, but it would not be too difficult to achieve something similar today using the photograph and photocopier method described in this project. Silhouettes work particularly well for fairy-tale characters and scenes; these are a suitable theme for a nursery wall, especially if they are made in bright colours.

You will need:

- Camera
- White background, such as a white board or a sheet
- Access to a photocopier
- Scissors
- Black marker
- Sheet of white paper
- Paper glue
- Picture frame

Method

1 Take a photograph of your subject's profile against a solid white background.

2 Photocopy the developed image at an enlarged size on good quality paper. (Normal photocopying paper will bubble up when stuck to a background.)

3 Carefully, with a pair of fine scissors, cut out your silhouette (**fig A**).

4 With a black marker, colour over the image so that it is solid black (**fig B**).

A

B

5 Glue the silhouette onto a sheet of good quality white paper (**fig C**).

6 Place in a frame of your choice.

C

MORE IDEAS

Silhouettes look pretty hung in a vertical line. You can link them by hanging a length of ribbon behind. Finish with a neatly tied bow at the top.

❖

Black-and-Gold Lacquerwork

The imitation of oriental lacquerwork has a long and rich tradition in the West. It is still popular today, and is used as a decorative technique for giving furniture a facelift. A number of highly colourful styles were used in the past, but the simplest for the amateur to imitate is gold-and-black lacquerwork. In this method, a design is applied in gold paint to a black background and the piece then given several coats of varnish to produce a very glossy finish.

The first examples of this type of lacquerwork reached Europe from Japan in the sixteenth century. The delicate gold brushwork and glossy backgrounds made a tremendous impact. Soon European craftsmen were producing similar goods in order to meet the huge demand. Its popularity was so great that, from the seventeenth to the nineteenth century, 'japanning' and 'japan work' became the generic terms to describe the many kinds of European lacquerwork that were inspired by the Orient.

The appeal of black-and-gold lacquerwork is that you can make the decoration as simple or as elaborate as you like. A simple first project is to lacquer a plain wooden chair. First of all, paint it black, then add small details in gold, such as a few simple leafy bamboo stems – a popular oriental motif. Apply these to the back and front of the backrest and, to complete the transformation, cover the whole chair with several coats of gloss varnish. Ideally, the decorative brushwork should be applied freehand to give it the spontaneity of the earlier pieces.

If you are nervous about painting freehand, you can always practice on paper first, or trace suitable motifs onto the black ground (pencil tracings show up well enough on black eggshell). Almost any piece can be decorated in this way – table tops, cupboard doors, boxes, trunks or chests of drawers – as well as smaller items such as wooden lamp bases, picture frames and trays.

You will need:

- Wooden tray
- Small tin of grey undercoat
- Small tin of black eggshell paint
- Paintbrush
- Design or illustration, preferably oriental, to copy
- Chinagraph pencil
- Artist's brush, no 1
- Gold paint
- Wire wool
- Gloss varnish

Method

1 If you do not want to buy a new tray, paint an old tray black. First paint it with a grey undercoat. Allow 6 hours to dry and paint over with the black eggshell paint. Again, allow 6 hours to dry.

2 Draw the design on the tray with a chinagraph pencil. You can either make up your own or copy one from a book or magazine. If you are feeling confident, you can attempt a whole scene such as the one in this example (**fig A**), or you could do something simple, such as a floral design.

3 Carefully paint over the pencil drawing with gold paint, using artist's brush no 1 (**fig B**).

A

B

4 Allow the gold paint to dry overnight. Once dry, rub over it gently with wire wool. This will produce an 'antique' effect (**fig C**).

5 Apply at least four coats of varnish. Allow each coat 3 to 4 hours to dry. In proper Japanese lacquerwork, up to twelve coats of varnish would be applied.

C

MORE IDEAS

An exotic background for lacquerwork is imitation tortoiseshell. This can be achieved by using a reddish-brown background with black markings and silver or gold decoration.

❖

Using Studs

Metal studs have been used for centuries, to decorate furniture and to hold fabric coverings in position. In the Middle Ages, tables and benches were sometimes covered with leather held in place with studs. By the seventeenth century, when upholstered furniture was commonplace, studs not only held the fabric in position, but were arranged to echo the beautiful shape of the chairs. Eighteenth-century chairs sometimes included a simple scalloped pattern marked out in studs around the edge of the seat. By the nineteenth century, studs had generally been replaced by elaborate trimmings that hid the upholstery nailwork. Nowadays, studs of various shapes and metal finishes are found in most department stores and specialist upholstery suppliers and can be used to decorate upholstered chairs and wooden furniture as an alternative to braiding. A plain wide wooden picture or mirror frame looks good with a straight or patterned border of studs. Use a small hammer to tap them into position.

Studding a Cigar Box

You will need:

- Wooden cigar box
- Small tin of grey emulsion paint
- Black marker
- Small tin of green eggshell paint
- 2.5 cm (1 in) paintbrush
- Selection of studs
- Metal glue

Method

1 Undercoat the cigar box with grey emulsion paint. Leave to dry for 6 hours. When dry, paint over with the green eggshell paint (**fig A**). Leave to dry overnight.

2 Using the black marker, draw a design for your studs on the box (**fig B**). In this example, we have chosen initials.

3 Once you are happy with your design, stick the studs in place (**fig C**). Leave the glue to dry overnight.

B

A

C

Studding a Diary

You will need:

- Fabric of your choice
- Scissors
- Fabric glue
- Metal glue
- Selection of studs

Method

1 Open the book and place it on top of the fabric. Cut around the book, leaving a 2.5 cm (1 in) border around the edge. Cut a diagonal line across each corner of the fabric border 2.5 cm (1 in) long, making four flaps. Pick up the book and fabric and turn them over. Make two cuts on either side of the spine, 2.5 cm (1 in) deep. Fold over and stick down the two side flaps and then the four top and bottom flaps. Cut the spine flap into a triangle and tuck it into the spine with a dab of glue. You must stick down the flaps when the book is open, otherwise the material will not be spread taut over the book.

2 Stick on the studs with the metal glue. If you want, you can draw dots with a pen where you want to place the studs.

MORE IDEAS

Revamp an old tin can with studs (see above). Simply remove the label and wash in detergent. Dry the can and stick the studs on in a design of your choice. The finished item makes an excellent pen holder. (Before you begin, make sure the can has no sharp edges.)

Hanging Curtains

When curtains were first used in the seventeenth century, they were always hung from a rod by rings. Their decorative potential was completely overlooked. They were not hung as a pair at first, but usually consisted of a single length of linen, silk or taffetta, which served to screen out sunlight and no more. It was left to bed-hangings to provide privacy and insulation at night. These were made of the heaviest and richest material that each household could afford, and were lavishly dressed and trimmed. This treatment was eventually extended to curtains and, by the eighteenth century, pairs of curtains were a familiar sight. These were often festooned or swagged and were finished with a decorated pelmet or valance.

The humble curtain rod was transformed into a highly decorative item that was often carved, gilded and finished with finials based on classical motifs such as laurel wreaths and animal heads. These were draped with generous lengths of material in a variety of styles, and often included a second curtain of a lighter material. The Biedermeier period, which flourished in Germany between 1820 and 1860, adopted a much more low-key approach, and curtains were once again simply hung from brass rods. As a variant, fabric was sometimes casually wrapped around the pole and combined with a blind.

Curtain treatments

Today, poles are made from a variety of materials, including wood, brass, steel and iron. They are also available papered, painted and stencilled. Finials range from a plain ball to beautifully carved pieces such as spear and arrowheads, pineapples, artichokes, shells and flowers. When choosing a pole, try and match it to the style of curtain.

Tabs – loops of fabric attached to the top of the curtain – are one way to hang curtains; they can match or contrast with the main fabric. A tassel or other decorative device can be added at the bottom of each tab. A slot-heading consists of a fabric sleeve that is ruched up along the pole. Spotted muslin looks pretty treated in this way, although any lightweight material can be used.

Although any curtain heading tape can be used for curtains on poles, the easiest curtains to hang are self-lined and have ties that can be attached either to the pole or to rings. Make the ties from the same fabric or use a contrasting material or ribbon.

Curtains with Ties

You will need:

- Enough calico to make one pair of self-lined curtains and ties
- Scissors
- Pins
- Sewing machine

Method

1 Measure your window and allow enough fabric for one and a half times the width of your window. Allow 10 cm (4 in) for the hem and 5 cm (2 in) to fold over at the top. Cut four pieces of calico to the length and width required.

2 Seam up the widths. Put two sides inside out and machine the sides together and then turn inside out and iron. Hem the base of both curtains. You now have two lined curtains, left open at the top edge.

3 To make the ties, cut strips of calico 100 cm (40 in) long, 7.5 cm (3 in) wide. Work out how many you need beforehand. Fold each tie in half widthways and machine as near to the edge as possible (**fig A**). Then fold the tie with the seam in the middle at the back, and iron flat.

A

B

MORE IDEAS

*Instead of making curtain
ties from the same fabric as
the curtain, use a completely
different fabric or ribbon
(see right).*

❖

4 Starting at one edge, you will
need to sew in the ties along the
top at 15 cm (6 in) intervals. Fold
each one in half and place between
each curtain and its
lining and pin **(fig B)**.

5 Turning in the raw edges,
machine along the top of the
curtain, sewing the ties in as you do
so. When finished, you can either
knot them or tie them in a bow over
the curtain rail **(fig C)**.

Decorating Fabric

Painting and printing on fabric opens up a world of decorative possibilities. You can use special fabric paints to paint free-hand, transfer designs with crayons and inks, or try batik work. Printing with blocks (see pages 26–27) and stencils are particularly easy ways to decorate fabric – the effects are almost magical. Any of these techniques can be used alone or in combination to decorate a variety of soft furnishings, including curtains, cushions, wall hangings, and bed and table linen.

As an introduction to painting fabric, why not try out your design first on paper with ordinary paints. Before you start to paint the fabric, stretch it tightly over a padded surface using low-tack masking tape (you should always do this when painting or printing on fabric), then transfer the basic outlines onto the fabric. A soft-leaded pencil – but not too soft – is ideal for this, and will wash out in the first wash. Now start painting!

If you are nervous about copying a very detailed pattern or creating one of your own in free-hand, transfer crayons and inks are a good alternative. They give you considerable control and are very easy to use. Draw or trace your design onto paper, then colour it in with the transfer crayons or inks. As soon as the colours are dry, place the paper with the coloured side down on the fabric and press with a medium-hot iron. Test out the colours on a scrap of the main fabric you are using first – they look positively dull on paper but turn into brilliant hues once they have been exposed to heat.

Batik

The Javanese are the acknowledged masters of batik. This form of decorating fabric involves the process of resist dyeing, in which the design is first drawn in melted wax, applied to the fabric with a brush or a tool known as a batik needle (this consists of a handle to which is attached a small metal cup finishing in a slender spout). The prepared fabric is then immersed in a cold dyebath: the wax resists the dye and the pattern is formed. The fabric may be waxed and dyed a number of times, building up layers of colour in ever more complex designs. The decoration will not reveal its full glory until after the final dyeing, when all the wax has been removed.

Batik

You will need:

- Plain cotton fabric such as calico
- Pencil
- Tray, board or frame for stretching fabric
- Drawing pins or nails
- Batik needle or brush, no 4
- Wax (we used wax made from 30% beeswax and 70% paraffin bought from a craft shop)
- Double boiler or two pans - one on top of the other – in which to melt the wax
- Cold-water dye
- Cold-water dye fix
- Plastic bowl or bucket
- Wooden spoon

Method

1 Using the pencil, draw the design onto the fabric. If you are not confident enough to do this free-hand, draw the shapes onto paper first, then cut them out and draw around them. The design used in this example is a person's initials within a wreath of leaves. If you want to copy this design, you can draw around real leaves.

2 Stretch the fabric over a tray or wooden frame and nail it down. You should nail or pin the top first and then stretch it vertically and pin the bottom, and then the sides. Make sure it is taut.

3 Place the wax into a double boiler and melt it over the hob. As soon as the wax bubbles, lower the heat. You must be careful as wax is very flammable. You need to make sure it is heated but not boiling.

4 Once the wax is completely melted, you can start the batik process. Dip your brush into the wax, making sure you do not pick up any excess. Carefully paint the wax onto the fabric following your design (fig A).

5 Once the wax is dry (it dries within seconds), unpin the fabric from the frame and crumple it up, so that the wax cracks a little.

6 Immerse the farbic in a cold-water dye bath for the period of time recommended by the dye manufacturer (fig B). You will probably need to leave it in the dye bath for about 1 hour. Dyes vary, so it is important that you read the instructions carefully. With some dyes you will need to use a cold-water dye fix. Check your brand to see if this is necessary. Regularly lift the fabric out of the dye bath; this will prevent dye gathering in its folds. Every 10 minutes or so, stir the water with the wooden spoon.

7 Take the fabric out of the dye bath and hang it up over a bowl to dry. Leave it to dry overnight.

8 When the fabric is completely dry, remove the wax by ironing the design between two sheets of greaseproof paper (**fig C**). A small residue of wax may remain. To remove this, you must dry clean the fabric.

MORE IDEAS

Sponging with a natural marine sponge gives a wonderfully soft paint effect that is perfect for covers for scatter cushions. Use just one or two colours of paint, putting a little paint of each in separate dishes. Gently dip the sponge in the first colour and randomly dab it all over the cloth. If you are using a second colour, repeat, overlapping areas of the first colour.

Cushions

Cushions are one of the least expensive ways of introducing colour, pattern and texture into a room. There is an enormous variety of fabrics and styles to choose from and they can be used to give a specific feel to a room – a few brightly coloured cushions combined with one or two Indian-print throws will give a room an oriental flavour, while the combination of a quilted piece of fabric or patchwork throw and some floral-print cushions will instantly cheer up a room.

Plain cushions benefit from some kind of trim, whether it is tassels, piping or fringing in a complementary or contrasting colour. Introducing a wide, patterned border will also lift a plain fabric like calico. Leave borders straight for a crisp look, scalloped for a gentle edge or frilled for an even softer effect.

In Ancient Greece and Rome, the fabrics for cushions were richly woven or painted, and in medieval times fabric was sometimes painted to imitate expensive woven items and tapestries. Nowadays, there is an excellent range of fabric paints available; these are easy to use and offer endless decorative variations. This method is especially useful if you want to tie in a cushion cover with a design elsewhere in the room. You can do this by painting freehand, using stencils or printing with blocks.

Appliqué is a traditional craft that requires a sense of design more than skill with a needle, and it works well on a small area such as a cushion cover or a larger floor cushion for children and teenagers. Appliqué involves sewing cut-out pieces of firmly woven fabric to a larger piece of material.

Appliqué Cushion

You will need:

➤ Self-patterned or fine striped fabric for cushion cover

➤ Patterned scrap fabric (we used curtain fabric)

➤ Scissors

➤ Needle and thread

➤ Pins

Method

1 Cut out the shapes you want from the fabric and pin the cut-outs onto the cushion cover. We have used a floral design.

2 Sew on the cut-out with blanket stitch in the following way. Insert the needle into the fabric 6 mm (1/4 in) from the edge with the needle pointing away from the fabric. Hold the thread under the needle point and pull the needle through, forming a loop along the fabric edge. Repeat all round the cut-out.

Painted Cushion with Rope and Tassels

You will need:

➤ Neutral cushion cover such as calico

➤ Design to copy

➤ Pencil

➤ Small pot of black fabric paint

➤ Artist's brush no 6 or 8

➤ Black and white wool

Method

1 In pencil, draw in your design on the cushion cover. Paint over the drawing with the black fabric paint. Leave to dry overnight.

2 Cut lengths of mixed or plain coloured wool. To make the rope border, twist six lengths of wool together. To make the tassel, take a 10 cm (4 in) length of wool, fold in it half, and bind the top about 2.5 cm (1 in) from the top. Sew on the rope border and tassels with wool.

Cushion with Ticking Border

You will need:

Fabric for cushion cover (we used ticking)

Scissors

Sewing machine

Needle and thread

Method

Cut the fabric to make the cushion cover, allowing an additional 5 cm (2 in) for the border and 1.3 cm (^{1}/$_2$ in) for the seam.

Pin the right sides of the front and back covers together and machine 1.3 cm (^{1}/$_2$ in) from the edge. You need to make a hook-and-loop, zipper, or envelope closure on the back cover.

3 Turn the cover right sides out and press. Mark the depth of the border with pins and then topstitch all around the pins.

MORE IDEAS

Lift plain calico cushion covers by sewing on wide borders of embroidered ribbon – either all the way round the cushion or just down two opposite sides.

❖

Inexpensive lace looks pretty made up into cushion covers. Back with plain coloured fabric to set off the lace.

Dyeing Trimmings

Dyeing fabric is such a simple decorative solution that it is often overlooked. Yet what could be easier when faced with a plain white or off-white fabric or trimming than to dye it your chosen colour. It will be transformed in as little as half an hour.

Ready-made hot and cold dyes for the home market are designed to be as easy to use as possible, and they produce excellent results. They are also cheap and widely available. Yet before the invention of coal-tar-based dyes in 1856, by the English chemist William Perkin, dyers had to extract colours from natural sources such as vegetables, bark and fruit. This was a time-consuming and sometimes costly task. Fixing the colour was an even greater challenge to the early dyers. Many natural dyes are not fast unless the fabric has been treated with a chemical, known as a mordant, which enables the fabric to take the dye permanently. Commerical hot and cold dyes do not require a mordant – simply ensure that the fabric is clean and free of any finish that might interfere with the absorption of the dye. Salt must be added to the dyebath (the amount is given in the instructions that come with the dye) and commercial cold dyes also need to be fixed after the fabric has been immersed in the dyebath.

Natural dyes

Although ready-made dyes offer excellent value for money, it can be fun to try natural dyes. While not always as strong or bright as chemical dyes, they produce far more subtle tones. Woollen fabric retains colour for longer than most other fabrics.

Tea and coffee are classic home-made dyes that are fast without a mordant. Vegetables produce subtle and attractive colours; the outer leaves of cauliflower, finely chopped and boiled for about for 15 minutes, will produce a gentle pink colour. Onion skins produce a strong yellow if they are heated in water for about 40 minutes, and the leaves and stalks of parsley will give a pretty yellow-green colour if they are chopped finely and heated for 20 minutes. If you use a vegetable dye, you will need to mordant the wool beforehand. The vegetable dyes mentioned above require a mordant of tartaric acid and alum. Generally, when mordanting wool, you need to simmer the fabric for at least two hours and then rinse thoroughly, starting with very hot water and then gradually using a cooler and cooler rinse. When you place the fabric in the dyebath, the water should be the same temperature as the last rinse. If using vegetable dyes, you must boil the dye solution.

A

B

C

You will need:

- ➤ 1 lt (2 pt) boiling water
- ➤ Plastic mixing bowl
- ➤ Two tea bags
- ➤ Wooden spoon
- ➤ Cotton fringe

Method

1 Boil the water and pour it into the mixing bowl. Add the two tea bags and allow to brew for a couple of minutes (**fig A**).

2 Immerse the fringe in the dyebath (**fig B**) and stir with the wooden spoon. Leave the fringe in for 10 minutes, turning the fabric from time to time to ensure it dyes evenly.

3 Pull the fringe out of the dye bath with the wooden spoon. It will have dyed a very light biscuit colour (**fig C**). If you leave the fringe in for 1 hour, it will dye a much darker colour.

4 Hang the wet fringe up to dry.

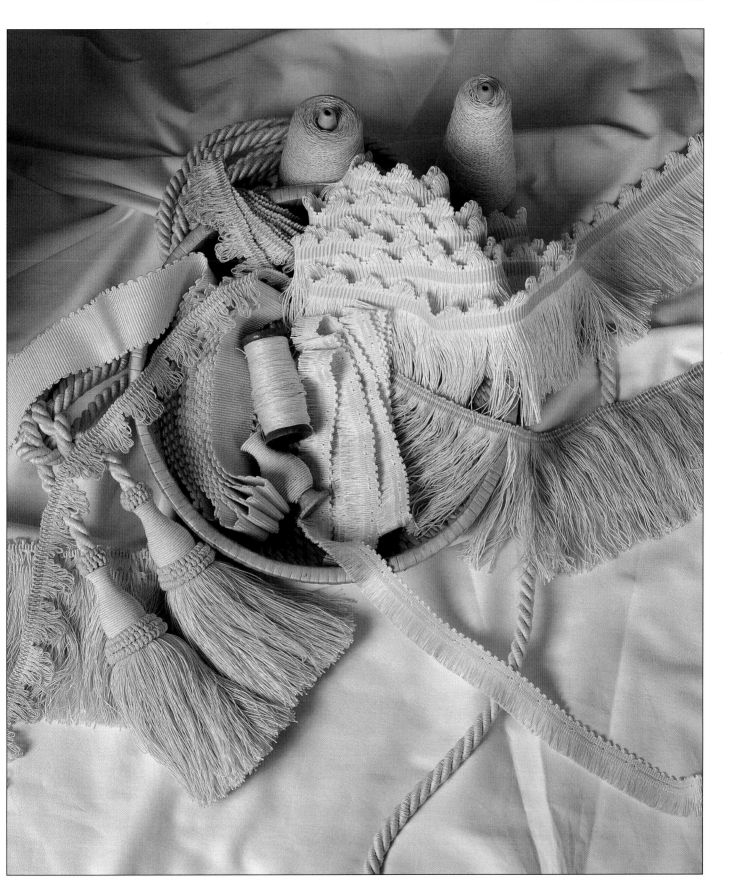